A THOUSAND ACRES

Dear Katy

Time now to read, &
write, plan, enjoy.
I hope so!

Love,
Manon

April 2017

A THOUSAND ACRES
writings from COUNTRY LIFE

CARLA CARLISLE

SNAKESHEAD
PRESS

Published in Great Britain in 2014 by
Snakeshead Press
131A Ashley Gardens, Thirleby Road,
London SW1P 1HL

in association with Mascot Media
(www.mascotmedia.co.uk)

A CIP catalogue record for this book
is available from the British Library

ISBN: 978-0-9540924-2-9

The Author and Publishers are grateful to COUNTRY LIFE
for permission to reproduce these articles

Editing and design: Marion Scott Marshall and Alan Marshall

Typeset in StempelGaramond

Printed in Great Britain by
Swallowtail Print, Norwich

This book is printed on acid-free Munken Premium Cream FSC paper

FSC is a non-profit international organisation established to promote the
responsible mangement of the world's forests. The FSC labels are independently
certified to assure consumers that they come from forests managed to meet the
social, economic and ecological needs of present and future generations.

CONTENTS

Introduction   *xvii*

I   TAP ROOTS

Holy Week   *3*

For Better, For Worse   *6*

Unequalled Nobility   *9*

Intelligent Silence   *12*

Attention Deficits   *15*

The Division Bell   *18*

A Duke's Farewell   *21*

Doves and Hawks   *24*

A Special Relationship   *27*

Bali H'ai   *30*

Perfect Safety   *33*

Wilful Testament   *36*

Rural Atlas   *39*

The San Pellegrino War   *42*

The Search for Heroes   *45*

Heaven's Maze   *48*

Mother Courage   *51*

Planet Sanity   *54*

Dearest Christabel... Darling Virginia   *57*

Foie Gras *vs.* Pork Rinds   *60*

A Patch of Pure Happiness   *63*

A Dose of Utopia   *66*

No Patriotic Strings   *69*

A Christmas Memory   *72*

II   FIELD MARGINS

Bird by Bird   *79*

Much Ado   *82*

Love Story   *85*

Vive La Chasse   *88*

The Easter Vigil   *91*

The Nightingale Prophecy *94*

Paying the Price *97*

Read All About It *100*

Cathedralist at the Showdown *103*

Hanging on to Awe *106*

Bending Towards Justice *109*

The Good Good–Bye *112*

Lifeline of the Countryside *115*

Are We Nearly There? *118*

Seeing is Believing *121*

Lives and Letters *124*

The Push of Time *127*

Laissez Les Bon Temps Rouler *130*

Simple Gifts *133*

Eggnog and Fruitcake *136*

III   CROP ROTATION

The Limousine Quartet *143*

The Pathos of Lost Things *146*

Books Revisited *149*

Swan Song   *152*

A Legacy of Truth and Justice   *155*

Gardener, Writer, Friend   *158*

Thoughts of a Melancholy Optimist   *161*

The Last Iceberg   *164*

In Loving Memory   *167*

Homeland   *170*

The Mockingbird Legacy   *173*

The Heart of the Matter   *176*

The Best of Robert Carrier   *179*

Reservoir Dreams   *182*

A Place for the Genuine   *185*

September Song   *188*

Civil War   *191*

IV   UNDER THE PLOUGH

Shopping and Changing   *197*

Silent Spring   *200*

The Green-Eyed Giant   *203*

List of Wishes   *206*

Reflections from the Lambing Shed *209*

A Savage Kingdom *212*

The Last Speech Day *215*

The Sorrow and the Pity *218*

Love on the Net *221*

Concrete Proposals *224*

Driving on the Right *227*

When Government Was Good *230*

Our Great Dame *233*

The China Syndrome *236*

Green Lite *239*

For Richer and Richer *242*

The Treadmill of Regret *245*

Comfort and Joy *248*

V   SEED CORN

Thrift or Re-Gift *253*

Optimism for Beginners *256*

Farewell to St James's Square *259*

Letter from Paris *262*

Life @ the Writer's Almanac *265*

And the Winner is... *268*

Lamentation for the Day *271*

Let Evening Come *274*

Alas, we have CCTV *277*

World Land Trust *280*

The Fire This Time *283*

In the Land of Bofus *286*

The Whistlejacket Redemption *289*

Manners Maketh Marriage *292*

Testament of Hope *295*

Home on the Range *298*

VI   LATE HARVEST

A Winter's Tale *305*

Letter from Washington *308*

Try to Remember *311*

The Meaning of Brown Eggs *314*

Between Grief and Hope *317*

More Chomp Than Chew *320*

Timewatch *323*

Common Good, Common Sense *326*

Country Life *329*

The Fog of War *332*

The Meaning of Treason *335*

Books: A Memoir *338*

The Snow Goose Prophecy *341*

Truth *vs.* Mercy *344*

The Habitat Advent *347*

Stay Hungry, Stay Foolish *350*

A Moveable Feast *353*

In memory of
Malva and Red
who did not remain silent

and for
Mac Gordon
a true friend and a good writer

INTRODUCTION

Southerners love hearing themselves talk. They tell the same stories over and over again. I've told the story of Nancy Astor returning to Virginia after her honeymoon and introducing her new husband, Waldorf, to her beloved Aunt Liza so many times that members of my family can lip-sync the old nurse's reply: 'Why, Miss Nancy, you sho' done outmarried yo'self!'

Because they know my stories by heart my husband and son are sometimes tempted to tell them too, but they can't do the accent or the timing. 'You know the lines,' I say, 'but you can't carry the tune.' Still, I appreciate their glazed patience as they listen yet again to the story of the oak tree at Wyken that is older than America or the origin of my grandmother's philosophy that 'manners are more important than brains'.

Those looks of familial tolerance haunted me as I gathered together a *second* collection of writings from COUNTRY LIFE. Is this taking Repetition too far? That same grandmother would snap 'don't preface every dish with an apology' when I began my culinary career, marinated in the Killing Code (we had to clean, cook and eat everything we shot, a countryside law that stopped us from shooting cats and king snakes). Instead of apologising I can only offer the excuse that the first collection appeared a decade ago and a lot has happened in the world since then.

For one thing, the son I wrote about in the early years of my occupancy on the back page of COUNTRY LIFE grew up. Although my original deal with him was mercenary – if I mentioned him in a column I owed him a pound – there came a time when I accepted the statute of limitations on using the child as column fodder.

And country life changed too. As I write this, the land on three sides of our farm has been bought by German industrialists. We aren't completely surrounded, but it brings a whole new meaning to 'pincer movement'. The most recent purchase is the farm next door which sold (according to the grapevine) for £15,000 an acre. We're still shaking our heads over that figure. I should add that we went to the bank every single time these farms came up for sale, fired up by that old mantra that you only get one chance to buy the land that adjoins yours. Back in 1989 we flinched at Bill Morley's land going for £2000 an acre. Now we feel pretty foolish about not being braver back then, but you don't have to be Einstein to know that at £15,000 an acre a farmer can never produce a legal crop that will even pay the interest.

There is one consolation to our economic cowardice. Keeping our farm to the size it is gave me a good title for this collection, although not an original one. You probably know it: *A Thousand Acres, A Novel* by Jane Smiley. Hers is the story of an Iowa farmer who decides to divide his 1000-acre farm between his three daughters. The story re-imagines Shakespeare's *King Lear*, and it's a book I love. Despite the fact that there is no copyright on titles (no title deeds), I only feel worthy of the title because I actually farm 1000 acres.

I'm grateful that the real farm where these columns were written is blessed with lighter soil (beneficiary of the ancient laws of primogeniture) than the treacherous topography of Miss Smiley's fictional farm. But there are no hedges so high, no farm tracks so winding, that you can ignore the world beyond your sacred boundaries. It is a world full of dangers and, despite every resolution of optimism, that troubled world appears in these pages more often than I remembered.

My spiritual guide during the years of writing these pieces was the writer E.B. White. Whenever I felt particularly stuck or bereft, I relied on him to dig me out. I kept his words taped to my desk: 'I discovered a long time ago that writing of the small things of the heart, the inconsequential but near things of this living was the only kind of creative work I could accomplish with any sanctity or grace.' White looked at the world through the lens of his saltwater farm in Maine, and the small things of his day – the behaviour of pigs, the price of hay, milk, eggs, land, gasoline – kept him from becoming overwhelmed by the big things which, in his case, included the Depression, Hitler, the Second World War and the atomic bomb.

I'm more at home with the narrow lens myself. The small things of my day – the birth of lambs, the cashflow of a vineyard restaurant, the frost on vines, the price of wheat, the companionship of chickens, the siren song of lovesick peacocks – and the small things of my heart – the people who work on this farm and the two men, my husband and son, who anchor me here – were the starting point of every column. The big things – Afghanistan, Iraq, floods, oil spills, financial crises – often meant that sanctity and grace were beyond the reach of my keyboard.

These miniature essays on country life were written in a period when the economic and political status quo was dramatically altered. I did not always have the serene self-confidence to say that I was right and that our leaders (and the bankers, the generals, the company directors and even the voters) were not only wrong but ridiculous. Still, I felt it was my bounden duty to be as vigorous and indiscreet as my back page piece of real estate would allow. I was blessed in having an editor who never once said 'whoa!'. I suspect there were times when he wanted me to turn down the Apocalyptic volume, times when he would have liked me to take my grandmother's advice – 'For Lord's sake, write something cheerful for this gloomy old world' – but Mark Hedges is one of those rare editors who believes that the personal freedom of the writer should win out and he sticks to his guns.

If they subscribe to COUNTRY LIFE in heaven, I reckon my grandmother was frequently disappointed. She too was a farmer, a Southerner who believed in blood more than intellect. She would not have been impressed by E.B. White's farming; neither would she have been moved by White's description of his hero, Henry David Thoreau, as a man torn between 'the gnawing desire to change life, and the equally troublesome desire to live it'. She was a dairy farmer, and when you are milking twice a day, every day of the year, you don't have time to chew over the meaning of life.

I've been lucky to have the time and arable tranquillity to speak out on things agricultural, cultural, religious, canine, bovine and moral. My only regrets are these: that I haven't been a little more cheerful and that I haven't changed the world.

Carla Carlisle

Wyken
October 2014

The country is the real thing, the substantial thing, the eternal thing; it is the thing to watch over and care for and be loyal to; institutions are extraneous to it, they are its mere clothing, and clothing can wear out, become ragged, cease to be comfortable, cease to protect the body from winter, disease and death.

- *Mark Twain*

Instructions for life:

Pay attention.
Be amazed.
Tell about it.

- *Mary Oliver*

I
Tap Roots

HOLY WEEK

EASTER in the countryside is a time of delirium. It is primal: the birth of lambs. It is lyrical: daffodils blowing hope against hope across the grainy green sea. And it is hard work. Rural dwellers who no longer charm the bank with their sugar-beet returns gear up for the prolonged harvest that begins at Easter: the crop of public. Teas and crafts in the barn, art galleries in the old stables, gardens and nurseries in ancient barley fields, weddings in the thatched tithe barn. It's an orgy of endeavour and it's how Fay Weldon describes creativity: 'Nothing happens, and nothing happens, and then everything happens.'

It now feels curiously remote, archaic even, but Easter used to have a different meaning. My father, moralist, Old Liberal, idealist, saw Easter as the mainstay of the religious year. He believed that Holy Week was the force that kept the whole Christian faith from falling into the void. As we sang our hearts out, he celebrated the single belief that made his spiritual life worthwhile: the Resurrection.

It is Easter week and I take my mug of coffee and Roberts radio to the garden where I listen to the *World at One*. I shoo the peacocks off the garden seats and begin the de-encrustation process so that next week's paying visitors won't feel gypped. It is spring 2004 and the language on the radio is a foreign one: Hamas, al-Qaeda, suicide-bombers. The militant pieties of Islam, Judaism and Christianity seem a world away from this corner of Suffolk where the sugar-beet factory (eight miles away) presides over our pastoral universe. But a mere 25 minutes from here, sprawling across acres of suburbanised prairie flatness, are America's two largest airbases in the UK – Lakenheath and Mildenhall. This Holy War – also known as the War Against Terrorism – has a giant foothold in East Anglia.

Of course, nobody round here talks about Holy Wars, terrorist threats or thorny theological tenets such as the Resurrection. Folks who come every Saturday to our farmers' market seek comfort in the wholemeal sourdough bread and free-range eggs, benediction in the fresh fish from Lowestoft, absolution in Jane Capon's organic Jersey cream. You can only worry about so much in life and, what with the scare over farmed salmon, the nightmare of the proposed IKEA warehouse in a village that is 10 miles from a major road and the futile fury at the gypsies who stole 600 metres of cable just delivered by Framlingham Farmers, believe me, there is enough to dwell on. Turn off the radio.

All the same, it seems a pity that the Resurrection has become a relic we've handed over to the fundamentalists, a notion that has no place in the intellectual, peaceful, law-abiding world of democracy, biology and physics. Without that crucible to hang our faith on, we become what my Pa called 'cultural Protestants'. We are a growing band. On Easter Sunday you will have to get to the cathedral in Bury St Edmunds early because it will be so full of us. I will examine the progress of the new tower, visit the sculpture by Elisabeth Frink, and feel grateful for this beautiful, serene and living holy place. (My father also called me a Cathedralist, which was not intended as praise.) Even as the communion wafer sticks to the roof of my dry mouth I will pray: for peace in our time, oh Lord.

April 8, 2004

FOR BETTER, FOR WORSE

MY husband sure does hate it when there is a death in my family. It's not because he sees that look of hurt and sadness in my eyes. It's because he gets worried. You see, in my family, on the eve of Significant Funerals, somebody comes out of the closet.

On the eve of Mama's funeral it was my cousin Elizabeth. She announced the happy news on the telephone to her mama, my Aunt Nita, who decided that this was a mourning too far and stayed at home.

On the eve of Pa's funeral, it was my cousin Jamie who told the family that her friend Susan was also her partner. This really was a surprise because Jamie was married to Bill for nearly 20 years and has four children. But my parents, devoted heterosexuals, were always seen as the Progressive Wing of the family. I reckon it felt right to take a stand on the occasions of their Liberation from Earthly Life.

Everyone in the family has more or less come to terms with this turn of events. In general it is agreed that it is better than the olden days when Uncle Sonny stayed in the closet despite several marriages and a pretty messy life. And, as far as I know, none of my gay cousins have registered silver, crystal and china patterns on www.weddinglist.com and sent out engraved invitations. In my family such restraint would be considered more a case of good taste than a moral attitude.

Weddings, gay and other, have been on my mind, ever since I learned that the Church's General Synod is considering reforms that would allow conventional couples to marry in any Church of England church they wish. As it is now, church weddings can be held only in the parish where either the bride or the groom lives or worships, unless the couple apply for a special licence. Since 1994 more couples have chosen 'approved premises' such as hotels and country houses as a venue for their vows. Church marriages have dropped by 40% in the past 10 years. It is common sense for the C of E to get the brides back down their aisles.

When we married, my husband and I had a dazzling choice of churches: the Victorian church in Putney where I was a Spinster of the Parish; St Margaret's, Westminster, where his parents and grandparents were married; the National Cathedral in Washington where I graduated from high school. We chose the Crypt Chapel of the Palace of Westminster for its medieval splendour and economic size. Although the bridegroom was an MP at the time, it required a special licence, a magnificent document that resembled Magna Carta and which we have now lost.

If you are prevented from marrying in the exquisite Norman church you loved as a child because you no longer live in the parish, if you cannot say 'I will' in the heavenly chapel next door to your reception, you will be tempted to opt for a civil ceremony. Greater flexibility may be hard on churches lacking architectural merit but I believe that the marrying couple should be able to choose the church where they become man and wife.

In the years ahead the Synod will get to dwell on the thornier issue of marriage and gender, but now is the time to take a stand on the principle of architecture. And my dear husband can relax: when it comes to gender *vs.* architecture, I go for architecture every time.

April 22, 2004

UNEQUALLED NOBILITY

IN a posthumous collection of essays and stories, the writer Carson McCullers describes her first reading of Isak Dinesen's *Out of Africa*. From the unforgettable first line – 'I had a farm in Africa, at the foot of the Ngong Hills' – to the last sentence of the first page – 'Everything that you saw made for greatness and freedom, and unequalled nobility' – Miss McCullers was hooked, dazed by the poetry and truth of that great book.

Because of *Out of Africa*, she loved Isak Dinesen. When Dinesen rode through a 'maise grassland', Miss McCullers rode with her. She read the book with so much love that its author became her imaginary friend. 'Although I never wrote to her or sought to meet her, she was there in her stillness, her serenity and her great wisdom to comfort me.'

And then, to her astonishment and joy, Miss McCullers was placed next to her at a dinner in Dinesen's honour at the American Academy of Arts and Letters. By then the

Danish writer was very frail and old, but 'her face was lit like a candle in an old church'.

At the dinner, Dinesen confided to her neighbour that she would like to meet Marilyn Monroe. Miss McCullers knew Marilyn, and Arthur Miller was at the next table, so a luncheon in Miss McCullers's apartment was arranged.

Dinesen was a magnificent conversationalist and loved to talk. No one liked to interrupt her. Marilyn, 'with her beautiful blue eyes' listened in a 'once-upon-a-time way'. Dinesen only ever ate oysters and Champagne, and at the luncheon Mr Miller mentioned the importance of protein and queried the wisdom of doctors who would commend such a narrow diet. 'Doctors? The doctors are horrified, but I am old and I love Champagne and I love oysters and they agree with me.'

That story came back to me last week when Alistair Cooke died. With his early-morning eloquence, his humane, compassionate, perfectly wrought and graceful perceptions, he became my imaginary friend. He never failed to comfort, amuse and enlighten me. Although I never wrote to him or sought to meet him, he was there, giving rhythm to my week, continuity and clarity to my life.

And then one day, to my astonishment and joy, I was placed next to Alistair Cooke at a small dinner in London. It was in the summer of 1984, in the home of Michael and Georgina Gill. Mr Gill was the brilliant producer and director of *Civilisation* with Kenneth Clark, a remarkable achievement in television that he followed with Cooke's *America*.

There were only five of us at dinner. Like Dinesen, Cooke was a wonderful talker. He sounded as succinct and relaxed as *Letter from America* – and only his wife, Jane, was at ease interrupting him. What I remember most was the elegance, the discreet cigarette between courses and his obvious affection for Mr Gill, whose *America* had provided Cooke with his first-ever prosperity. I have the awful feeling that I listened in a 'once-upon-a-time way'. I never saw him again, but you could say that we faithfully kept in touch.

Time spent in Alistair Cooke's company – and that is what *Letter from America* was – felt like a telephone call from home. It improved my view of America and of being an American. I think it also improved my view of the Universe. I'm grateful for all those years we spent together, and I will miss him for a long time.

April 15, 2004

INTELLIGENT SILENCE

STUPIDITY in a woman is unfeminine. That's what my grandmother drummed into her granddaughters during the long summer days when we were abandoned to her care. She said it when we slept late (past milking time, which was not late) and when we read *Seventeen* instead of Daphne du Maurier. She said it when we preferred horses to piano, poker to bridge. I associate the sentiment with her so utterly that I was amazed to learn that Nietzsche said it first, in his essay *Human, All Too Human* in 1878, a work my grandmother certainly never read. Although her principal desire was to conquer our stupidity, she accepted the inevitable patches of ignorance. For these moments she urged us to cultivate an 'intelligent silence'.

Stupidity has been on my mind since the Easter holidays, when Sam organised a family quiz. The questions were provided by *The Field* under the heading 'Are You a True Countryman?'. The contestants were Sam, 15, second year at Harrow, main passions in life: shooting and fishing; my husband, farmer, council member of the Royal Horticultural Society, main interests in life: saving the grey partridge, beetle banks, ancient woodlands, wildflower meadows; and me, born and raised on farms (cotton, soya beans, dairy) and, for the past 17 years, on this Suffolk farm (wheat, barley, sugar beet). My main passions? Chekhov, Jane Austen, Eudora Welty, Bach, Brahms, Aaron Copland, Keith Jarrett, Shetland sheep, Dark Brahma chickens and (*write* it) cities.

The quiz consisted of 50 questions. We began with our photocopies, pens and kitchen timer. Even with my smart-aleck acuity and rural roots I didn't really expect to win. I predicted an 'English bias' but I was confident. I believe that acquiring the language of the countryside is something that happens naturally, a gentle osmosis.

Well, dear reader, do you know how many eggs a pigeon lays? The three names of the stages of the young salmon between its emergence from the egg and the time it reaches the sea? A Bedfordshire clanger? How you count hounds? The name of the mating dance of the black grouse? The 'frog' on a horse? Husband and son managed to score 'True Countryman Born and Bred' although they were not at the top end. I barely made it into 'Townsman whose Heart is in the Country'. I avoided 'Stay in Chelsea' by two points.

I think it's important at least to try to speak the language of the country you live in, but I think there may be two Countryman languages, like Swiss German and German

German. It may be further evidence of my stupidity, but I'm making a quiz for the countryman who lives on Cold Comfort Farm circa 2004. I'm looking for answers to the following questions: What is Defra and how is its money spent? How long will shooting last if fox-hunting is banned? Is Britain the only country in Europe making no effort to encourage a land-based green energy policy with biofuel crops? How many people a year leave farming in this country? Do we really want a countryside covered in houses? How much of our milk now comes from Poland? When are we going to wake up?

I'm looking for answers even if I am a countrywoman whose heart wanders. Even if my femininity would be enhanced by an intelligent silence.

April 29, 2004

ATTENTION DEFICITS

I AM sitting in my restaurant with my cousin Elizabeth. She is in England on a tour with her church choir and has made the two-hour train journey to Wyken on her only free day. I have not seen her for nearly five years, a tumultuous time during which her father died, she has moved house, become a successful psychotherapist and had a few fallouts with her siblings.

The couple at the next table have been waiting a long time for their main courses. The party of six have their wine but not their bread. Across the room a queue is waiting for tables in the café.

Elizabeth stops talking and looks at me. 'I'm going to tell you what I tell my patients. *Be present with me.*' The words cut to the quick. *Be present with me.*

For the next hour I practise being present with my cousin. It is not easy. For one thing, I am sitting in my own restaurant and I am so used to taking in every detail (water in vase on bar needs changing; new waitress has noisy shoes; ceiling fans turned up too high) that I have to turn my chair inward so that I cannot see the room. But the main problem: I am out of the habit of giving anyone my full attention. It demands concentration. It requires effort, patience, goodwill.

It is St George's Day and the CLA is hosting a breakfast for 60 of its Suffolk members here at Wyken. The Lord Lieutenant of Suffolk is seated on my left. Tim Tollemache is a friend whose company I love and he is telling me about a fascinating trip to Jordan he recently took with his family. At the end of the breakfast I remember only a fragment of the story. Was I really listening or did he give up on the effort to get me to be present with him?

I call to check on an old friend who is in a rocky marriage. While we are speaking she says: 'Hold on a sec.' I hold until I realise she is scanning her emails while we talk. I start to say: 'Hey, be present with me.' Instead, I cut the conversation short and hang up. But how prickly can I be? How many times have I said: 'Can you hold, it might be Sam on the other line...'?

The truth is, Attention Deficit Disorder is the disease of our time. It is not a problem confined to hyperactive children wired up on sugary foods and computer games. It is a plague that has infected everyone who is upright and functioning. Even in the dozier world of country life, we live in an omnipresent anarchy of mobile telephones, emails, post piles and remote controls. When there are moments of quiet calm, we clutter the silence. I walk into the kitchen to fix dinner, a peaceful moment at last. But before I pour a glass of wine, I turn on the radio, the over-the-counter Ritalin that tranquillises me just enough to get the salad washed, the vinaigrette emulsified.

I have decided to really work on the art of listening. I realise this cannot be a mere hobby, that being present is a full-time occupation, occasionally exhausting but frequently rewarding. I feel like the country mule who first must be whacked to get his attention (Be present with me. *Whack*!). I have already discovered this: one real conversation gives you a sense of tranquillity, like a long, quiet walk through the woods. Could you hold just a sec – that might be Sam calling.

May 6, 2004

THE DIVISION BELL

THE Bank Holiday Monday was half over when my husband realised that it was the 25th anniversary of his election to Parliament. It was appropriate that the anniversary snuck up on him because his election victory had snuck up on him, too. He was fighting the traditional Labour seat in the City of Lincoln. Although Dick Taverne, now a Liberal Democrat peer, had briefly shaken up things there in 1972, Lincoln had been Labour since the war. My husband, a Suffolk farmer, was fighting his first unwinnable seat, that essential step on the ladder to a safe seat closer to home. His opponent was incumbent Margaret Beckett (Jackson she was then). He won Lincoln by 600 votes and didn't get to bed that night until 3am because Mrs Beckett demanded three recounts. Disbelief is a time-consuming emotion.

Still, I felt the anniversary called for a celebration, so I put a bottle of Champagne in the fridge, took a pheasant from the freezer, harvested a bundle of asparagus and washed my hair. It was chilly and wet, but we sat in the apple orchard drinking and remembering. His main memory is one of shock. He didn't expect to win and hadn't made plans. His first telephone call was to his parents who had only seen 'Recount in Lincoln' flash by on the television screen. His next call was to his farm foreman to arrange a meeting first thing the next day.

All this now seems strangely remote, not because a Conservative victory feels historic, but because the political landscape has been transformed in the past 25 years. Nowadays, a farmer and a bachelor would have a slender chance of being selected as a candidate. Other drawbacks – Harrow, Oxford, fifth-generation Member of Parliament (the first three generations were Liberals) – might sink him long before he made the shortlist.

So what has changed in this quarter of a century? For one thing, there is a new breed of politicians, men and women who have been in politics all their lives as officers in white-collar trade unions and local government. On the other side (okay, the Conservative side), there is a silent recognition that the old avenues of life – Parliament, Foreign Office – are tightly shut. The ancient notion that being born with privilege incurs a debt (call it service) is over. With the life of service excluded, the life of making money has become the principal alternative. And no, I don't think that making money simply became more attractive, although historically it was a pragmatic prelude to parliamentary careers. My husband's annual parliamentary salary in 1979 was £3,000. A good potato crop enabled him to make a down payment on a small flat within the division bell.

Liberal and Conservative phases follow each other in a succession of waves throughout history. I think it important not to allow gloom to settle in your heart, but I worry that a House of Commons with no farmers is precarious and unsatisfactory. Our future is determined by folks who do not understand that civilisation depends on a living depth of topsoil, that climate will have a bigger impact on human ideas than the stock market. I'm sitting next to a farmer who thinks hard about the economics and irrationalities of global food production, a man who knows that water will become the new oil. His old opponent, Mrs Beckett, is Secretary of State for Environment, Food and Rural Affairs. Go figure.

May 13, 2004

A DUKE'S FAREWELL

I HOPE you saw the photographs in the *Daily Telegraph* of the funeral procession of the 11th Duke of Devonshire. Against the deep honey-coloured stone of Chatsworth House stood men and women dressed in the proud uniforms of their professions: chefs in their whites and billowing toques, housekeepers in the mysterious insignia of half aprons and full aprons, young men in white shirts with black armbands and, carrying the Duke's coffin on their shoulders, sturdy gamekeepers in their estate tweeds. For the 600 staff who followed the route for the Duke's funeral, it was a personal tribute to a generous, reliable, good-natured employer. For those of us who love common sense, the English countryside and the endangered terrain where history and tradition converge, it was also a farewell.

This is goodbye to a Duke who never expected to be a duke, who had a mere six years to get used to the idea, from the wartime death of his elder brother in 1944 until the sudden death of his father in 1950. Farewell to a Duke who faced such crippling death duties – 80% of the value of the Devonshire estates – that he spent 1 7 years struggling to save Chatsworth for the family and for a nation that should be forever grateful that it is not another 'cultural institution,' a northern offshoot of the V&A or a National Trust property where visitors would search in vain for signs of the true spirit of place.

By his own admission, the supremely intelligent Duke was 'lazy beyond belief' at Eton and Cambridge (raise your hand if you think he would even get into Eton and Cambridge today) but, like many men of his generation, he was transformed by the Army and the Second World War into, as he put it, 'something vaguely approaching a man'.

He was also transformed by his wife, the Mitford sister whose nursery songs included 'Someday My Duke Will Come', a true countrywoman who called her Duke a 'town yob'. Resident Sane Voice of the countryside, the Duchess is a rare blend of beauty, brains, fun and shrewd tolerance.

In truth, the tall, lanky, immaculately dressed 11th Duke was just about everything a duke should be. A Duke who loved both the company of women and the slightly shabby masculine world of his clubs; who loved the Turf but was passionate about books and modern pictures; who loved the land but believed that landowners who fought access and the right to roam were intolerable. 'They will lose in the end and therefore they should lose gracefully, willingly and at once. It's a question of goodwill.' A Duke who was wisely Eurosceptic, believed that the Scottish and Welsh had too much power in Westminster, and lamented the ever-increasing divide between town and country. A Duke who deplored the city people who wanted the countryside to become a theme park. 'The indigenous industries in the Peak District are quarries, but city folk don't want quarries. Do away with the quarries and you do away with jobs. Do away with jobs and you do away with communities. It's that simple.'

They say that when a man dies, a whole world dies with him. The 11th Duke of Devonshire takes with him a world that has already begun to fade into memory. There was no eulogy at the funeral, but no eulogy was needed. It is there in the photographs. Save them, if only to line a drawer. Save them for another generation to discover and gaze at in amazement.

May 20, 2004

DOVES AND HAWKS

SAM has started calling home almost daily. He begins with a casual mention of schoolwork. 'What do you know about the Cuban Missile Crisis?' he asks, and patiently listens. 'Well, it was scary. We thought there was going to be a nuclear war.' Then he gets to the real reason for his call: 'Any activity in the kestrel nest?' This is a boy who dreams about hawks.

I'm not sure when the passion began. Maybe with the tawny owl he rescued from the sheeps' water trough when he was nine. Perhaps when he read and re-read T. H. White's classic *The Goshawk*. There have been times when the enchantment seemed dormant, eclipsed by fly-fishing and the pheasant season. But last summer, the obsession grew. He went on day-long falconry courses. He spent long hours practising his falconer's knot, and a term's pocket money on a leather gauntlet. He revelled in the influence of falconry on the English language: a 'bate' is a hawk's tantrum; a 'mews' is a hawk's night quarters; 'unreclaimed' is a hawk that has gone wild.

Now he yearns for his own hawk. Last summer he found a kestrel nest in a hollow ash tree near the vineyard. For weeks he kept a silent vigil, sometimes honouring us with a private view. From his secret post we watched bald baby kestrel heads peeking out, waiting for their *prêt à manger* to arrive. And we discussed the pros, cons and methodology of kidnapping a baby kestrel.

I wasn't put off by the illegal nature of kestrelnapping. My resistance was more personal. The diet for a start. The early feeding regime of birds of prey is more restrictive than the induction phase of the Atkins diet. Young birds are fed deep-frozen day-old chicks, but if they gain – or lose – two ounces in a day they can die. Daily weighing of your hawk is vital. Daily bathing is strongly advised. And then there is the training, a labour-intensive process that demands unlimited commitment of time and patience.

Tonight's telephone call starts again with the Cuban Missile Crisis. He has an essay to write and he wants to know about the Bay of Pigs. I tell him right away that there is still no sign of Mama Kestrel returning to her nest. Silence. Then I launch into an account of the week-long doomsday in 1963, the battle between the hawks and doves in President Kennedy's cabinet, the blockade that ended in a rare victory for the doves.

'And the Bay of Pigs?' he asks. I explain that it was

25

two years earlier, and attempt a condensed version of the cockeyed plan concocted by the CIA for the invasion of Cuba by Cuban exiles. I tell him the CIA assured Kennedy that they would liberate Cuba from the dangerous tyrant Castro and bring democracy to Cuba. That the grateful Cubans would dance in the streets. As I speak I can hardly believe my memory. Historical fiasco. Bad intelligence. Fatal ideology. As Yogi Berra put it: 'This feels like *déjà vu* all over again.' I then remember another small splinter of history. Ten days after the Bay of Pigs debacle, the Department of Defense presented Kennedy with a report outlining how Vietnam could be 'saved'. It was approved.

Hawks are aggressive and powerful birds. They are instinctive hunters. But to train them you have to be as pacific as Gandhi. Power is countered with gentleness, tantrums with patience, pain with kindness. Studying the Cuban Missile Crisis is fascinating, but perhaps falconry should be compulsory.

May 27, 2004

A SPECIAL RELATIONSHIP

FOR months I boycotted the new Ottakar's Bookshop in Bury St Edmunds. We already had a wonderful bookshop, owned by Stephen de Sautoy and his wife, a literary bookshop lined with black-and-white photographs of W. H. Auden, Marianne Moore, Elizabeth Bishop, Seamus Heaney. I was afraid that Ottakar's would kill it off, and it did.

The New Saxon Bookshop is now a café, and I have succumbed to Ottakar's. I visit every week or so, put together an ecumenical stack of books and go upstairs for a cappuccino and an economical edit of my pile. Which is how I wound up with John Mortimer's *The Summer of a Dormouse*, a slim, two-hour paperback that is like sharing a good bottle of wine with a gossipy, witty friend.

The passage that moved it to the 'yes' pile takes place in the bar of the Royal Court Theatre, where Mortimer meets Seán O'Casey's daughter, Shivaun. He recalls that Harold Macmillan was best friends with O'Casey's widow, took her out regularly and urged her to marry him after his wife died.

Mortimer misses that healthier political age when it was possible for a one-time Tory prime minister to want to marry the communist widow of a communist playwright. Shivaun tells him that her father much preferred his Conservative friends to his communist friends who were, she says, quite frankly a pain in the neck. His principle was to vote with the left but to have dinner with the right.

You could say that I am a relic of that healthier age. A child of the Sixties who veered so far to the left that I wrote my history thesis at Princeton on the 'Economic Success of Marxism in the Soviet Union' (a work of dubious scholarship), scrapped the idea of law school and went to work in factories that were points of production for the war in Vietnam. I packaged lethal defoliates in the optimistic belief that, once enlightened, I would convince the workers of the injustice of the war; and, once enlightened, they would down tools. My fellow workers, many with sons in Vietnam, were remarkably cheerful, kind and tolerant, whilst my leftist comrades, suspicious of my tomato plants, bantams, love of wine and sense of humour, were a pain in the neck. Perhaps it was an extreme step to marry a Conservative Englishman, but in future I will just cite the O'Casey principle.

This story preoccupies me because all week I've been listening to the D-Day broadcasts on the radio. I've felt that familiar pull of political schizophrenia: hating the war in Iraq and wishing like crazy that Blair hadn't legitimised Bush by giving this country's support, and feeling soul-shaking gratitude for the alliance of America and Britain 60 years ago.

Although it took place before I was born, the story of D-Day is part of my life and time. My mother's first husband and the father of my sister was one of the young American soldiers who left these shores and landed on Utah Beach. He survived Normandy but died six months later in the Battle of the Bulge.

As The Queen bids a last farewell to the D-Day generation, I am sitting in an English garden, books and wine at my side, listening to her English voice tell those selfless soldiers of our eternal and 'immense debt of gratitude'. I think of that world-saving alliance: in sorrow and in awe. I am grateful.

June 17, 2004

BALI HA'I

MY friend Susie from Maine is in London. She and her sister Amanda have brought their father and his oldest friend Paul over for a theatre week. The two widowers are in their eighties, and the trip would be impossible without their two girl guides: Paul, as creative and brainy as he ever was, is nearly blind, and Roderick, affectionately called Papa Loco by his four grown children, has Alzheimer's.

In a feat of logistics they come to Wyken for the day. We have lunch in the garden, then I take them back to the train in time for *South Pacific* at the National Theatre.

Throughout their visit Papa Loco talks very little but seems to be enjoying all the chat that whirls around him. He is thin, dapper, shy, sweet. The next day Susie calls to report on the evening. 'He sat in silence on the whole journey back, then, in the middle of the overture a big smile came over his face. Suddenly he said, "Bali Ha'i"'. Ah, the joy of recognition that passeth all understanding.

Since then, 'Bali Ha'i' has become our euphemism for

Alzheimer's, senior moments and total fadeouts. I tell this story to the regular visitors to the garden, farmers' market and café who bring their still-portable loved ones here, the husbands, wives, fathers, mothers who have moved from daylight to twilight and are now resident in nursing homes in Stowlangtoft and Ixworth.

'Bali Ha'i' has become such a part of the Wyken vocabulary that I instantly thought of it when I heard that Ronald Reagan had died. He was never the president I loved. Too much an actor reading his lines to seem presidential to me, too fond of anecdote, I never saw him as the President who restored America's post-Vietnam confidence. But my Democrat heart softened when I saw his handwritten letter in the papers in 1994 telling of his illness: 'I now begin the journey that will lead me into the sunset of my life.' What a wretched journey.

I felt sympathy too for Nancy Reagan, who called her husband's Alzheimer's 'the long goodbye'. The woman I thought played the over-the-top adoring political wife became a human being when she told how she had hoped that her constant presence would snatch him from the meaninglessness of Alzheimer's, when she wrote about the disorder and oblivion that marked her husband's dying and death. I came to admire her as she fought for embryonic stem-cell research, putting her at odds with the Republicans who had once adored her. 'Ronnie's long journey has finally taken him to a distant place where I can no longer reach him. Because of this, I am determined to do whatever I can to save other families from this pain.'

Last week, a cluster of family and friends gathered here at the restaurant after a memorial service for a woman who had died of Alzheimer's aged 64. I studied the service sheet that was left behind. It included Psalm 103 that speaks of God's mercy: 'Who forgiveth all thine iniquities; who healeth all thy diseases; who redeemeth thy life from destruction; who satisfieth thy mouth with good things; so that thy youth is renewed like the eagle's.' I didn't know the woman but I wondered at the choice of reading. I tried to think of what I would have chosen in its place but no words came to mind. Only the memory of Papa Loco's smile. Bali Ha'i.

June 24, 2004

PERFECT SAFETY

IT comes as no surprise to me that the word 'travel' comes from the Latin 'trepalium', which, loosely translated, means 'instrument of torture'. The older I get, the more sedentary I become. 'A trip up the Amazon? You go, darling, I'll stay home and look after the dogs.'

So, back in March, when an invitation arrived from New York for the 80th birthday party in June of an old friend, I looked at it anxiously. Then I started to think about my friend, who is one of the most remarkable men I know.

I first met George Lang in the late Seventies at a dinner at Johnny Apple's flat in Eaton Place (better known to his friends as Eatin' and Drinkin' Place). Then bureau chief of the *New Tork Times* in London, Johnny was a prodigious host, famous for bringing together unlikely combinations of people, food and wine.

On that evening, a fellow guest, an impeccably elegant man, arrived late, amusing us with his story of going to the wrong address. We were instantly mesmerised as he told us about his day spent buying a Stradivarius violin. But his audience did not know half the story: George, the only son of a Hungarian Jewish tailor, was destined to be a concert violinist until, at the age of 19, he was incarcerated in a German forced-labour camp. Miraculously, he survived by passing himself off as a tailor. While George mended uniforms, his entire family – mother, father and all his grandparents – were sent to Auschwitz. They never returned.

Over the years, our paths crossed in Paris, Rome and New York. Although he introduced me to my first white truffle (Rome), he revealed little about his life. I learned some of the facts at a dinner in New York when I sat next to his friend, the writer Elie Wiesel, a fellow Hungarian whose accounts of surviving Auschwitz won him the Nobel Prize. And I learned more from George's wife, Jenifer, who pushed George to write his memoir, *Nobody Knows the Truffles I've Seen*, a moving account of his childhood, his harrowing experiences in German and Russian labour camps, his escape from Hungary into Austria, finally reaching New York, where he surrendered his dream of a musical career and became a restaurateur.

When we met, George had already resurrected New York's Café des Artistes, giving it the unique culinary kiss of life that he would later bestow on Budapest's landmark restaurant, Gundel's.

These stories dance in my head as I arrive at the party. I watch George greeting friends: ageless, elegant, happy and a little bewildered. In the midst of the gathering of the beautiful, the great and the good, I see George and Jenifer's shy, pretty 13-year-old daughter, Gigi, and their tall, poised 17-year-old son, Simon. George was only two years older than Simon when he slipped three slim books into his pockets as he left for the unknown world of labour camps and war: the philosophical writing of Epictetus; poems by Arpád Tóth; and Epicurus's *Ethics*.

George once told me that the ideals of Epicurus provided him with the leitmotif of his life: that nothing terrible lasts for ever and, within the boundary of life and its tragedies, the most perfect safety is friendship. I make a private toast to Epicurus and to George. How lucky we all are to be here. This is a journey *vaut le voyage*.

July 1, 2004

WILFUL TESTAMENT

I WAS touched and a little surprised when Aunt Patricia left instructions for us to arrange her funeral. For one thing, she has a son and daughter, even if they do live a long way from Suffolk. Also, she's never really approved of us. Still, my Southern genes are never so alive as when planning a final farewell, preferably for someone who has reached their ninth decade but has enough family and friends left behind to make a good funeral. By which I mean: nice food, plentiful drink, distant relations who understand the heart's hunger for homecomings and the potent pleasure of a good laugh and a good cry in your best clothes. Some shops stock bestsellers such as *The Nation's Favourite Love Poems*. My shop stocks *Do Not Go Gentle: Poems for Funerals*.

One decision had already been made. Aunt Patricia was already at the Co-op Funeral Services because the friends with her when she died peacefully at home knew that the austere Liberal Democrat-Soil Association-Samaritan octogenarian wanted honourable and basic. While my husband (Patricia was married to his father's brother) went to get the death certificate, I spoke to Susan at the Co-op.

If she was disappointed when I requested 'cheapest' she didn't show it. (Mind you, the Co-op basic is £1,646: £700 for professional services including the hearse; £110 for death certificate; £375 for crematorium; £310 for basic veneer coffin.) I asked about bio-degradable cardboard or willow coffins, but the Co-op has not gone green. I knew that Aunt Patricia, a dogmatic vegan and fierce environmentalist, wouldn't approve of artificial brass handles and pine veneer but I had to agree on the spot because Susan had managed to get a 'slot' at 9.45am on Friday at the crematorium at Risby. 'You're so lucky. Some families wait for weeks.'

Before you could say, 'We brought nothing into this world', I had chosen hymns and readings, filled the house with food, printed the service sheets on recycled paper and picked garden flowers for the coffin. I was memorising Jane Kenyon's *Let Evening Come* and brushing the dog hairs off my black Jaeger suit when the telephone rang.

It was Patricia's son John calling to say that they had nowhere to stay. Her solicitor and executor informed them that, as they are not the principal beneficiaries, they were not allowed entry into the family home; that her son would receive £1,000, her daughter a meagre amount more, grandchildren nil, great-grandchildren nil; and that

37

no one can see the will until it goes to probate – which can take at least six months. Through stealth and chance we learned that the cottage, contents and land are left to the Vegetarian Society.

Somehow I got through the service. I served steak sandwiches at the wake and rare roast beef and leg of lamb at the family suppers. I ransacked our house to give the grandchildren stuff that had belonged to the great-grandparents, to compensate for their grandmother's cruel lack of generosity. But nothing I could say or do could erase the bewildered grief, love and hurt on the faces of Patricia's two children, who have never known anything like the financial security her parents-in-law had provided for her.

Meanwhile, I am looking for a book to add to my shelf of funeral literature, a volume to lean against John Donne and Philip Larkin. I want something along the lines of *The Idiot's Guide to Contesting Wills*. Until I find it, nobody is going to rest in peace.

July 8, 2004

Note: The will *was* successfully contested.

RURAL ATLAS

A POEM by U. A. Fanthorpe that I love, a tribute to her partner, Rosie, begins:

> There is a kind of love called maintenance
> Which stores the WD40 and knows when to use it;
> Which checks the insurance, and doesn't forget
> The milkman; which remembers to plant the bulbs;
> Which answers letters; which knows the way
> The money goes; which deals with dentists
> And Road Fund Tax and meeting trains,
> And postcards to the lonely; which upholds
> The permanently rickety elaborate
> Structures of living; which is Atlas.

I wish I had written it for my husband. I did give him a copy, but his eyes glaze over when he sees slender columns of poetry the way mine glaze over when he presents me with the farm accounts. Marriage is accepting these defects in each other, and good marriages are the ones in which the defects and the talents are not duplicated.

In this marriage we do not duplicate ability on any front. I don't balance a cheque book and he doesn't stir-fry. In the garden I am Harold and he is Vita. I specialise in vistas, seats and paint colours. He is a genuine plantsman. The only plant name I am sure of is *Fremontodendrum californicum*, and I flaunt it at every opportunity.

Even our private yearnings could hardly be more different. My idea of the perfect holiday is somewhere with sidewalks, cafés, galleries, bookshops and museums. I like the greenery to be under control: magnificent flowers in the hotel lobby; parks filled with foreign children, good sculpture and fountains that work. My husband likes botanical trips with like-minded folk, ambitious journeys spent outdoors that often feature the same meal every day for two weeks.

But it is this stretch of temperaments and desires that has enabled us to transform a sleepy arable farm into an estate worthy of the Royal Agricultural Society's Bledisloe Gold Medal. Usually I'm the one who hogs the limelight, with tales of my apocalyptic vision of English farming that pushed us to plant the vines, convert the 400-year-old barn into the vineyard restaurant and shop and create the weekly farmers' market. But the truth is, my husband was the one who made sure that forms were filled in, letters written, bills paid, bank managers and planners placated. And at the same time as he was bearing the burden of tedious, demanding administration, he was quietly following his bliss: creating wildflower meadows from seeds he painstakingly collected from meadows that have never been sprayed in the history of the planet; creating beetle banks, conservation headlands, a lake that is a wildlife habitat, nurturing ancient woodland, planting thousands of new trees.

Sitting in the sun and watching the Duke of Gloucester present the medal to my husband, my mind wandered to the photograph that hangs above my desk. Eudora Welty is presenting the American Academy of Arts and Letters Gold Medal for Fiction to William Faulkner. On the back is a quote from her speech. 'Mr Faulkner, I think that the medal, being pure of its kind, the real gold, would go to you of its own accord, and know its owner regardless of whether we were all here to see or not. Safe as a puppy it would climb into your pocket...' My feelings exactly.

July 15, 2004

THE SAN PELLEGRINO WAR

MY friend Katie is so small and naturally skinny that she has never paid VAT on clothes. For years she wore Sam's 'Gap Boy' jeans when he outgrew them, and she still sleeps in his old T-shirts. When I tried to pass on the one that says 'Support Your Local Hookers', she saw through my maternal deceit and promptly mailed it back to Sam at Harrow.

A few days ago she arrived with her manual Hermès typewriter, her wind-up radio and her sleeping bag, an L. L. Bean Explorer that she lined with her mother's chinchilla coat the year she died. In summer she sleeps on top; in winter she snuggles inside. Katie opposes the fur trade, but she felt that no animal would be saved if she buried her mother's endangered but dead coat.

I am never quite prepared for Katie's visits. I get in her usual supply of soy milk and she sniffs: 'Soybeans are now genetically engineered in ways that are fatal to biodiversity. Drinking soy milk does not help cows.'

42

When Sam was small and still loved McDonald's, she bought him a Happy Meal. As he ate, she explained that the little bitty quarter pound of beef in his burger had required 100 gallons of water, 1.2 pounds of grain, more petrol than his container of Coke, the same greenhouse-gas emission as a one-way trip to Bury from our farm and the loss of 1.25 pounds of topsoil, every inch of which takes 500 years for the microbes and earthworms to build. Sam finished eating before solemnly anouncing, 'I do not believe this cow died in vain'.

Now Katie has a new cause. She is trying to interest *Panorama* in her script about the 'real cause' of the war in Iraq. 'All this talk about weapons of mass destruction. It *never* was that.' We nod knowingly.

'No,' she says. 'It's time the world understood that this war is about Perrier. Badoit. Highland Spring. Evian. Volvic.' She looks me in the eye as I try to hide my bottle of delightfully still Hildon water. 'San Pellegrino!' she snaps.

She begins her purposeful message: the British now drink almost two billion litres of bottled water a year. Americans have passed the trillion-litre mark. The energy required to make the plastic to contain the water, and the fossil fuel used to deliver it to the supermarkets and back home to our kitchens is the equivalent of a year's oil production from the North Sea.

'It's a racket. We've been conned into thinking we need eight glasses of water a day, that to detox our bodies the water has to come from a bottle. All bunk. We're washing away all the nutrients from our food with this Niagara Falls intake of water. All those expensive vitamins you take? Flushed out before you can say 'snakecharming is killing the planet'.

I look wistfully at my bottle of Hildon water. I love its Gauloise blue label and I love its taste. At least I think I do.

'It's more expensive than petrol! It's double the price of milk! You shouldn't sell it in your restaurant. Just Say No.'

Katie has been refilling empty Hildon bottles at the kitchen sink all week. My husband has calmly replaced Hildon with martinis. Still, some of our customers look confused when they see the banner hanging over the bar: STOP THE WAR: DRINK FROM THE TAP.

July 29, 2004

THE SEARCH FOR HEROES

I DON'T know what it is about summertime that makes me feel like I have to be serious because nobody in the Carlisle family likes it. I blame it on the English system of sending your beloved offspring to boarding school and letting complete strangers take on the job of instilling values. When these cherished sons and daughters come home at half-term, Christmas and Easter, we are too busy treating them like returning war heroes, indulging their every desire – and gently trying to get them to come clean about what homework they are supposed to do.

Summertime is our only chance to give them a crash course in how to live, how to allocate their time, how to be happy, how to love. ('Whoa,' says Sam when he hears this tone in my voice, 'I'm not running for president, you know.')

For a long time the hope of my summer seriousness was to find a hero for Sam, someone who would excite and inspire him. That was my aim a few years ago when we made a detour on our trip to Maine and spent a day at the Kennedy Library in Boston. I know that Kennedy was flawed, but I wanted to conceal the defects long enough for Sam to be fired up by the man who was the hero of my generation. The library, housed in the majestic I. M. Pei building overlooking Boston Harbour, tells the compelling life story of the 35th president of the United States: war hero, writer, politician, president. If it is history at its most edited, it is also history at its most edible.

Sam was moved by it all: photographs of the PT-109; recordings of the inaugural address, the letter written by the future president aged 10 pleading for an increase in pocket money, a report card that gave no sign of academic distinction.

A few weeks later Sam was spending an evening with his godmother. After supper they watched one of those *Timewatch* programmes on BBC that revealed all about JFK. The next morning an anxious 10-year-old voice said to me: 'Mama, I think there are some things about Kennedy that you don't know...'

I have continued my search for a hero. Sam now has so many books on Churchill that he grimaces when he sees one coming. He admires Martin Luther King, but the Baptist minister who preached non-violence is a remote role model. Right now, Sam's idea of a hero is someone who has been clever and earned lots of money (à la Google) and goes fishing in Iceland, Russia and northern Patagonia.

Freedom, justice and saving lives does not enter into it.

This rainy summer, my quest for heroic material seems confined to trips to the cinema. My recurring message is: making it in life requires diligent effort and deferred gratification. After seeing *Fahrenheit 9/11*, Sam points out that George W. Bush showed neither diligence nor deferment before the age of forty 'and look at his job'. *Shrek 2* (the fifth top-grossing film of all time) is a sensitive green ogre who proves that goodness and courage are inner qualities.

But *Spider-Man 2* addresses the issue head on. 'Everybody loves a hero – people line up for them,' Aunt Mary tells Peter, the geeky, untidy, hopelessly disorganised college student who, when duty calls, becomes Spiderman. On the way home, Sam says he thinks I missed the point. 'When Peter dumped his arachno leotard and stopped saving the world, he got his homework done on time. What is the message in that?'

August 19, 2004

HEAVEN'S MAZE

A FEW summers ago we had a birthday party for Elizabeth, my mother-in-law. I should say my late mother-in-law, because it would have been her 90th birthday. The party seemed like a good idea for many reasons. For a start, it was an excuse for her children and grandchildren to wander in the maze we had given her for her 80th birthday.

As a girl growing up at Bodnant in North Wales, Elizabeth had loved designing mazes, but her designs had never left the page. Thrilled to think that she would finally have a living maze, she started work immediately, producing 20 designs. Then she was diagnosed with liver cancer. She spent her last few months poring over her designs with my husband before making the final choice. She chose copper beech because 'yew is too formal for a field', and insisted that it be only shoulder height, a maze for children. A few weeks after her death, on an icy December morning, my husband staked out her design into the frozen earth. Ten years on, the dense beech hedges were just what she intended: 'challenging but not menacing'.

The birthday party was really a family reunion: her only sister, her younger brother and her son and daughters. We drank Wyken wine in the maze (named 'Heaven's Maze' by her three-year-old grandson) and told our favourite 'Elizabeth' stories, many about her driving which led to regular court appearances. She always arrived dressed immaculately in her St. John's Ambulance uniform, telling the clerk that she was due at Covent Garden and would it be possible to appear early. It worked every time.

The first-born child of a glamorous mother and a preoccupied father, Elizabeth suffered the affliction of her time: the invisible heartbreak of parental neglect. She camouflaged her pain well, aided by the competitive McLaren gene which she confined to Scrabble, backgammon and bridge. Her quick, mathematical brain collided with a lifelong suspicion of higher education for women, this despite the fact that her sister Anne went to Oxford, became a world-famous geneticist and Fellow of the Royal Society.

Marriage rescued Elizabeth from the pressure to be as beautiful and witty as her mother. She once told me that 'the nicest thing about marriage is that you don't have to make conversation'. When Peter, her husband, inherited Wyken there was no question of coming here to live. She loved London: bridge, movies, theatre, friends, a base for grandchildren. Country houses were for weekends and holidays. After Peter died, she was relieved that she had stayed at Airlie Gardens, insisting that 'London is a very nice widowhood'.

Shortly after my marriage, we planted an avenue of bee-friendly limes connecting the garden to the woods. David Kindersley carved the slate plaque on the gatepost, which reads, 'For Peter Carlisle who loved Wyken these trees were planted'. At the unveiling we stuck a homemade plaque on the opposite gatepost: 'Paid for by Elizabeth who loves London'.

Early this summer we had another birthday weekend for Elizabeth. This time I realised what I like most about these gatherings. They challenge the notion that when you are gone, you are gone. However much the meaning of our lives is fixed with the living, there is still a vibrant patch reserved for those we have loved and for those who have loved us.

August 26, 2004

MOTHER COURAGE

IT must be nearly 20 years since I saw *The Assam Garden*, the film in which Deborah Kerr plays a woman whose husband has just died. The couple had run a tea plantation in India and on their return to England he creates an elaborate Indian-style garden. Miss Kerr resents his obsession. She is convinced her husband gave his life to it. As a widow, however, she tends his garden: mowing, watering, weeding, planting.

I thought of the film this week in Scotland when I saw Jean plucking grouse on her own in the gun room at Dalnaspidal. This was Roger's job, performed in solitude while the guns and their wives, weary from the day on the hill and dozy from tea and great cakes, sought hot baths and rest before dinner. Roger used this time to review the day: where there'd been plenty of grouse, where the heather was looking sparse, which dogs were good, which dog owners were a menace. I reckon Jean was reliving the day in silent conversation with Roger.

It is one thing to nurture India in an English garden, but the challenges that face the widow of the laird of a large Scottish estate fall into a whole other category. When we all returned to Dalnaspidal last year, our first time there without the exuberant, larger-than-life Roger, we arrived with solemn foreboding that this might be the last gathering of the happy, motley clan that annually walks these hills, shoots enough grouse to justify the huge effort of preserving their habitat, eats wonderful food and tells the familiar stories that bind us together. We couldn't believe that Jean would take on the immense and lonely burden of running the estate on her own. Her two children passionately love Dalnaspidal but they are in the early stages of artistic careers (translate: no City salaries) and, however great the emotional commitment, the financial reality of these estates is overwhelming.

But none of us had reckoned on the Deborah Kerr in Jean Adams. She tackled the financial challenge of Dalnaspidal by selling the family home in Essex and making the lodge her full-time home, along with a herd of protective labradors. Soon both children followed, James transforming the Smithy at Blair Atholl into a sculpture studio, and Fiona and her husband travelling and writing from their base in Glen Lyon.

And, with granite determination, Jean began another battle after Scottish and Southern Energy announced plans for a new power line rising 165ft (twice the height of present pylons) to service Scotland's proposed wind farms. Jean – who has turned down offers from three wind-farm companies – learned that the proposed route zigzagged across the heart of the wilderness of Dalnaspidal simply 'to lessen the visual impact of the giant pylons from the A9'.

She fought off the original plans that would have devastated hundreds of acres of wild and totally unspoiled moorland beloved by hill wallkers. New 'options' are between the existing route along the east side of the A9, and across the road onto the magnificent, unspoilt hills of Dalnaspidal.

I don't think that SSE know what they have on their hands. This is a woman fighting for an ancient patch of wilderness and for the memory of the man who loved it, a woman who believes there must be limits to the human footprint on this earth. When the time comes for a remake of *The Assam Garden*, I'd suggest *The Hills of Dalnaspidal*.

September 2, 2004

PLANET SANITY

I'M standing in the village post office with a package to send to Sam. Fortnum & Mason Ceylon tea bags. The slippers he left behind. Tucked in the toe of the slippers: a jar of Tiptree Little Scarlet strawberry conserve and a bottle of Camp coffee. A boarding school care package.

In front of me in the queue stands a woman I know by sight but not by name. Her large box barely fits on Hilda's scale. It's also for her son, and she tells us it contains boxes of cereal (Cheerios), loo paper, Vaseline, shaving cream, dried apricots, socks, the new anniversary edition DVD of *E.T.* We laugh about mothers and sons. She then tells us that her son is in Iraq, in Basra.

Late last night, while husband and dogs slept, I called my friend Nicholas in Maine. His son, a 46-year-old married professor, is in the Iraqi city of Najaf with his California National Guard unit. Every month his friends and family send him packages: sun block, lip balm, T-shirts, tinned meat, razors, CDs, magazines, gun lubricants, snuff.

54

Gun lubricants? Snuff? 'Yes,' Nicholas tells me calmly. 'Snuff is excellent for bartering. And there is a chronic shortage of ammunition and gun lubricant. Unfortunately, we can't send bullets.'

This summer my son confessed to me that he had never really liked the movie *E.T.* I couldn't believe it. When Sam was small we watched the film about a group of Earth children who help a stranded alien botanist return home 10 dozen times. It's a magical film about friendship on earth, love and loyalty, adventure and miracles, life and death, trust and treachery. I find myself thinking about it as I leave the post office because I wonder what that affectionate, loyal Extra-Terrestrial would think if he landed in Backyard Planet Earth today. What would he make of a war fought with the most sophisticated and lavish weaponry ever devised by man, a war that began with Shock and Awe, and now has mothers and fathers sending loo paper and gun lubricants to soldiers who are trapped in a quagmire of urban warfare?

I continue the *E.T.* test as I walk across the fields where our farm manager is ploughing. The sight of a confetti of seagulls trailing the John Deere tractor against the dark earth usually fills me with peace and hope, but today all I can think about is a world gone haywire. Soldiers without basic necessities whose government has spent more parliamentary time debating foxhunting than it has spent debating Iraq, terrorism, health care and jobs put together. A Prime Minister who placates his Labour members who opposed the war by tossing them the bone of a fox-hunting ban. A country in the hands of politicians who, with astonishing enthusiasm, accept foxes as a trade-off for keeping our soldiers in the hostile, lawless land we've created.

In the movie, E.T. longs to get back to his own planet but, in a scene of heavy-handed shock and awe, the government authorities who want to capture him kill the small wrinkled alien. In the denouement, that hair-raising chase with E.T. in the basket on Elliot's bicycle flying in front of the moon, a barely resurrected E.T. reaches his compatriots just in time for the trip back. Maybe E.T. has a message that I missed all those years ago. I hear a voice in my head and it's saying that it is time for us to return to the planet of sanity. The planet of humanity. Come home, it says. Come home.

September 30, 2004

DEAREST CHRISTABEL... DARLING VIRGINIA

'LIFE would split asunder without letters,' Virginia Woolf wrote in *Jacob's Room*, her third novel. When it was first published in 1922, Virginia Woolf had already written at least 1,200 of those life-saving and saveable letters.

Nowadays, life would split asunder without email. Without it I would scarcely be in touch with family and friends, but what a gigantic hole looms in our literary ever-after. Letters are the time capsule, the patchwork quilt, the spark that survives the blur of time. Virginia Woolf's letters gave me England and Englishness, at least that part of it that was civilised, unsentimental, liberally inclined and thrilled by the intelligence of young artists and writers: the Englishness of Bloomsbury.

How exciting it was back in the mid-seventies when those letters first began to appear. On each visit to London I would make a pilgrimage to John Sandoe's bookshop off Sloane Square to purchase the latest volume. I spent nearly a decade of winter evenings sobbing over the death of her young brother Thoby, helping her sister Vanessa find a cook, raising money for T. S. Eliot so he could get out of the bank, starting the Hogarth Press ('We find we have only 50 friends in the world – and most of them stingy,' she writes to Ottoline Morrell. 'Could you think of any generous people?').

When Nigel Nicolson died in September I felt the need to revisit my Virginia Woolf shelf. The letters, the five companion volumes of diaries, the novels, the essays have lain dormant for the past 10 or so years, years when guilt at my own opus of unwritten letters, together with the fractured concentration of my email brain, have turned whole rows of books into countries I once knew well but now need a visa to enter.

I had just made it to 1922 ('Writing is still like heaving bricks over a wall...' she writes to E. M. Forster) when my husband's uncle, Christopher, arrived here for the weekend. 'I think I've brought you this just in time,' he said, handing me a slim booklet: Bulletin No 15, from the Virginia Woolf Society. On the cover is Cecil Beaton's photograph of Christabel Aberconway, mother of Christopher, and grandmother of my husband. Inside is the correspondence between Virginia Woolf and Christabel. It is the largest number of unpublished Virginia Woolf letters since the appearance of the six-volume *Letters of Virginia Woolf*.

I never met Christabel, who died in 1974, but I've always loved the family stories of this passionate society hostess described by Virginia Woolf as 'lovely, seductive, enchanting', who yearned to be with people who 'created and used words – writers'. I think she would be pleased at her posthumous starring role and amazed that her letters to and from Virginia Woolf have been given the permanance of print. These letters may lack the lucid, acute sensitivity of Virginia Woolf's correspondence with Vita Sackville-West and Violet Dickinson, but they are fascinating details on that vast literary tapestry.

Virginia Woolf wrote that the human soul orientates itself afresh every now and then. In that light, I type in www. virginiawoolfsociety.co.uk to print off the membership form. Bulletin 15 reminds me how much we will miss the letter writers. Christabel was sadly prophetic: 'No one writes long letters, letters giving news and gossip to country friends, nor do country friends send back long letters full of news to town dwellers. I doubt very much if people today even write long love letters.'

October 14, 2004

FOIE GRAS *VS.* PORK RINDS

I no longer remember when I learned that 'Cholmondeley' was pronounced 'Chumley' or 'Buccleuch' was 'B'cloo'. It was after I'd figured out that the Duke of Devonshire did not live anywhere near Devon and before I learnt that a letter to the wife of a lord was addressed to 'The Lady So-and-so' and not just plain old 'Lady So-and-so'. I still recall my astonishment when my friend Nicholas suddenly became Sir Nicholas Brooksbank, Bt. His wife, Emma, granddaughter of a hereditary peer and daughter of a life peer, shyly explained to me about baronets, a title that is hereditary but not noble. (And now they both have tucked their titles away into one of those timeless drawers filled with old shooting gloves, menu cards, engraved flasks with missing lids and other souvenirs of *temps perdus*.)

Even more confusing is the name change when aristocratic son succeeds aristocratic father, with titles sloughing off like snake skins. If Robert Cecil has an entry in your address book, you will have now scratched out 'Cecil' (pronounced *sisel*) and entered 'Robert Cranborne', scratched out 'Cranborne' and entered 'Robert Salisbury' – who is the Marquess of Salisbury in writing but Lord Salisbury otherwise. But don't take my word for it: I am in the same boat as the lucid and loveable Raymond Seitz, former American ambassador to the Court of St James's, who confessed that he never addressed an envelope with confidence.

Americans like to brag that our revolution freed us from the labyrinthine, brooding complexity of the English class system. We claim to value folks who create their success over those who are members of the lucky sperm club. We love looking at those shacky little birthplaces of Presidents Johnson, Reagan and Clinton because it props up our belief in the American dream.

But just lately it seems that we may have been too cocky about our classless pride. This presidential election has revealed that 'class' fits American feet as perfectly as a pair of shoes from Lobb's.

Not since the Second World War have two candidates been so alike: sons of privilege who both went to what Americans call prep school (and the English call public school): George Bush to Phillips Academy where he was head cheerleader, and John Kerry to St Paul's where he founded the debating club. They both attended Yale University, a Gothic universe inspired by Oxford and Cambridge, and in their final year they were both members of the secret society, Skull and Bones.

But, as is the way with caste systems of the well-born, there are opaque but important differences between the two. Kerry, progeny of the Winthrop and Forbes families, son of a diplomat, fits into the pinstripe mould of Eastern Establishment Brahmin. Bush, grandson of a senator and son of a president, yanked off his New England pedigree, acquired a Texas accent (not from his mammy and pappy, who speak pure Connecticut, complete with subjects and verbs) and went for the heehaw of Western culture.

When class and privilege are neck and neck, you expect the distinctions to be as obscure as, say, viscount *vs.* earl, White's *vs.* Brooks's. In the US election, the cultural divide has been cast as a choice between *foie gras de canard* or pork rinds, *Les Noces de figaro* or *High Noon*. But the real difference is more serious. We've made a mess of the world, and what we desperately need is a Prince of Peace. That's a title that shows no signs of being hereditary, but it will always be noble.

October 21, 2004

A PATCH OF PURE HAPPINESS

THE Grand Nieces Club met this week. Between us, our journey clocked up more than 15,000 air miles. We flew from our various houses in England, California and Maryland to New Orleans. After a night on the town, we rented a Cadillac, tucked our 'Kerry' buttons inside our pockets, and headed to a hamlet outside a small town in the middle of Mississippi.

We came 'home' to celebrate the birthday of our Aunt Edna, the only one left of the powerful trio of women who ruled our childhood. Our grandmother died 10 years ago, aged 93, in the rambling and decrepit house built by my grandfather. Aunt Blanche celebrated her 100th birthday and died three months later. Now Aunt Edna, youngest of the six daughters of Addie Alabama and Nathaniel Barnes, is 99. If character is destiny, it's right that she's still living at home. Five years ago her house was sold to a couple who hoisted it off its foundations and moved it down the road to Harperville. In its place is a pretty, comfortable house built by her daughter-in-law Ruby, a house where everything works and Aunt Edna is still in the middle of her beloved garden. It's the same, only better.

My sister, cousin and I grew up in the era when our grandparents were still on farms, but our parents had begun the long exodus from the land. As soon as school was out we were sent back to those farms for the summer, places that seemed far off and estranged from the rest of the world. This was before the Cult of the Child, when every day is planned – for three months nothing was ever planned. We lived in a world of cousins, heat, dogs and invention. The only rules were: 'Y'all stay outside', and 'Watch out for snakes'. The most attention we got was the nightly inspection of our sweet-and-sour bodies when red bugs were squeezed and ticks were pulled off.

But there was one patch of pure happiness in our lives: Aunt Edna's house, an oasis of love and shade. Even her front porch with its big porch swing was shady, and inside were cool, dark rooms and a permanent breeze.

Aunt Edna was the chief telephone operator in town. She knew who had gone into labour, whose septic tank was backed up, who was having female trouble. While she was at the telephone company and Uncle Ham was off fishing, we would enter her kitchen where there was always a fresh pound cake in the cut-glass cake stand, and a pitcher of sweet iced tea on the counter. We must have left crumbs and sticky glasses, but Aunt Edna never fussed at us: she believed in the absolute goodness of children, a belief that nurtured our gargantuan love for her.

Aunt Edna's mind and memory outshine our own. She still sits up straight as a dancer and likes to wear a 'touch of red'. Her only complaints: she's almost totally blind and she's outlived both her children.

In her honour, the Grand Nieces wear red scarves. Throughout the day more than a hundred folks come to pay tribute, but in the evening it's 'just family' – about 30 of us. We have our ritual family reading of poems and love letters we've all written to Mimi, our pet name for her. We're all tearful, but she just smiles. 'Y'all keep those chicken-feather wings. You have sent me straight to heaven and I'm still sitting here.'

A recent study of centenarians revealed that healthy 100-year-olds are remarkably un-neurotic. They don't brood or dwell on things. Maybe that's been Aunt Edna's message to us all our lives, but what I remember most is her soft voice telling us: 'Be sweet, angel hearts. Be sweet.'

October 28, 2004

A DOSE OF UTOPIA

THE Paris of my *jeunesse* was the 14th *arrondissement* on the Left Bank. My metro was Alésia, one stop from the desolate end of the line (Porte d'Orleans) and home was an uninsulated *atelier* that previously had been used for storing market carts.

Paris is a northern city, on a latitude with Newfoundland, and my memory of those days is of the pursuit of warmth. Like Hemingway, I spent many hours in cafés thawing out with a *petit crème*. Unlike Hemingway, I hated the smoke, found his courteous, warmhearted French waiters to be a myth, and the invasion of *les flippers* – pinball machines – a tragedy. I slowly discovered the *haut* world of the Right Bank, home of the Tuileries, the Champs Elysées and, world inside a world, les grands hôtels. Dressed like Jean Seberg, I would wander into these citadels of elegance and aim for a discreet, comfortable seat. I'd glance expectantly at the revolving doors before slowly taking out my notebook. After several hours I would return to *ma vie bohème*, restored and content.

My passion for les grands hôtels of Paris was like an unconsummated love affair: I flirted but I never stayed the night. On our annual October half-term trips *à deux*, I convinced my son that money was always better spent in good restaurants than on hotel rooms. Then, in one of those flashes of realisation – that the days are numbered when a 15-year-old willingly shares a room with his mother – I decided to go for broke. Instead of three days we would stay two, travel lowest fare Eurostar, walk everywhere, and stay at my dream hotel: Le Georges V.

My impression of George V was that he was notoriously stingy, a stranger to culture and hard on his children. The Avenue Georges V was named for the British king as a thank-you in 1924 for Britain's support during the First World War. The hotel opened four years later. In my youthful 'hotel' days, this was my absolute favourite and I was heartbroken when I heard that it had been refurbished and become the Four Seasons Georges V. But two years ago we had drinks with friends who were staying there. It was ravishing. Sam and I have yearned to go back ever since.

Despite the fact that guests look more like Jude Law and Bill Gates than J. P Morgan and Mr Frick, Sam and I dressed up for our arrival. At the reception desk we were greeted by Grace, a glamorous young woman who showed us around our deluxe suite. When I complimented her impeccable

English she smiled: she read modern languages at Bristol.

As soon as we were alone, Sam and I let out whoops of delight. This was paradise: a vast sitting room with views of Paris; a bedroom with two beds laden with cushions and goosedown pillows; a bathroom with ceiling-to-floor marble, a walk-in shower, a bath with shelves to rest your elbows.

Problem is, if you aren't to the grand hotel born, you never want to leave the hotel. Favourite haunts such as Angelina's and Ladurée looked shabby in comparison, and the surliness of *les serveurs* was a bore after the genuinely warm service at the hotel. We kept heading back to the hotel, me to the tapestry-lined gallery for tea, Sam to the spa. After we had dinner in the hotel restaurant, Le Cinq – now a Michelin three-star and the most beautiful dining room I know – we wanted to cancel our other reservations: we knew we had reached the top.

Sam did not improve his French (except for 'folie de grandeur'), but his appreciation of things French sharpened. He observed that Parisians have more pride than Londoners. In my favourite Paris bookshop, Galignani's, on the rue de Rivoli, I skimmed the political autobiography of the mayor of Paris, Bertrand Delanoë, *Life, Passionately*. The 54-year-old mayor's description of what makes a city great applies equally to a grand hotel. It is 'passion, and a dose of utopia...'.

November 4, 2004

NO PATRIOTIC STRINGS

ONE of the drawbacks of having a farmers' market on your farm is that a trip to Waitrose makes you feel like one of those evangelical preachers caught at the Brief Encounter Motel with somebody they aren't married to. It's hard to be the person who preaches the gospel of buying local when you love nothing more than a fridge full of yuppie lettuce, those wildly expensive bags of wild rocket that you just sprinkle into the bowl. I justify my faithless heart by saying that I've just popped in for loo paper, light bulbs and dog food. But nestled under the boxes of arborio rice and organic couscous is living food, some of which suggests air miles. I passionately love our farmers' market, but as Tammy Wynette sort of said: 'Sometimes it's hard to be a woman, giving all your love to just one *anything*.'

I've just returned from Waitrose, where I was thrilled to find shelves laden with baby pumpkins, cranberries and sweet potatoes. When I first came to England these items were available only in tins at Harrods, so I do not take for granted this abundance of Americana right in the middle of Bury St Edmunds. Beside this remarkable little crop was a poster with a soft-focus image of bounty, and in large letters: THANKSGIVING. Oh, Lordy. The Prime Minister now wears Levi's and cowboy boots and kneels at the altar of togetherness with George Bush, but this is crazy. Thanksgiving is not English. It's not even Harvest Festival. It's a celebration of the first harvest of the Pilgrims in 1621.

And here's a sectarian little footnote in case you're interested: the Pilgrims weren't the Puritans. The Puritans wanted to reform the Church of England – to purify it, hence the name Puritans – but the Pilgrims wanted to separate from the Anglican church. The small band of separatists who landed at Plymouth Rock in 1620 were the Pilgrims. The great Puritan migration came later, between 1629 and 1642, when life under Charles I became intolerable for them.

Waitrose is a meditative place, and somewhere between Fair Trade coffee and organic tea I began to reflect. Of course, the English should have a Thanksgiving, too. I recognise the signs of longing. Our vineyard restaurant has celebrated Thanksgiving since we opened 12 years ago and it is our most popular day of the year. And now that farm workers are an increasingly rare breed, and harvest ends in hot, summery August (except for the inedible sugar beet), the harvest festival has dwindled into a soppy-sweet service on the primary school calendar.

So I would like to propose an English Thanksgiving. A mostly secular day with no military or patriotic strings attached. No Dimblebys or Queens, just families gathered together without the pressure of giving presents, feeling grateful for a country that is still one of the most beautiful in the world. A country whose citizens are mostly honest, literate and courteous.

Deciding what to eat on English Thanksgiving won't be difficult. What's more English than roast beef and Yorkshire pudding or a really good curry? The tough nut to crack will be English cynicism and its cousin, pessimism, character traits that I suspect I have acquired after living here for so long. I have to push myself to remember that life really is good, and, in any case, it's not a dress rehearsal and it will only be as good as we can make it. Meanwhile, this Thanksgiving I'm upping the bourbon in my sweet potato casserole and hanging on to the words of the Scottish artist Alasdair Gray, painted in gold letters on a beam in a Glasgow church: 'Work as if you live in the early days of a better nation.'

November 25, 2004

71

A CHRISTMAS MEMORY

HARD as I try, I can't come up with any memories of my family drinking hot chocolate, listening to Bing Crosby and decorating the Christmas tree. I know that's what happened in television families, and I have friends who claim those memories, but when I poke round the memory bank nothing comes up. I have vague echoes of my mother complaining to my father that the tree was too short, too thin, one-sided, already dead, but it stops there. And that's because my mother waited until we went to school or to choir practice or to friends. Then she would pour herself a glass of eggnog generously laced with bourbon, put on an Ella Fitzgerald LP and decorate the tree. All by herself.

Every Christmas she chose a colour theme. I remember the pink-and-silver Christmas and the green-and-gold Christmas, but the one I liked best was the Russian blue Christmas. In the evening when we returned home, she would proudly present to us the tree that she had created with all her considerable, if somewhat frustrated, artistic talent. It was always perfect, always beautiful. Another thing I don't remember: ever telling her so.

I think of this template now as I pour my eggnog laced with bourbon. I poke the fire, put on the CD of the King's College carol service and then, all alone, begin opening the sea of boxes that contain a lifetime's collection of crèches.

The oldest crèche is carved from wood. It was made in the hills of Kentucky, where carving is called whittling, and Joseph, Mary and Gabriel all look like Abraham Lincoln. One year, before I realised that the crèche was the kind of folk art now collected by The Smithsonian Institution, I bought paint samples from the Shaker shop and gave Joseph a robe of Old Barn Red, Mary a gown of Cabinetmaker's Blue and Gabriel wings of Linen Cupboard White. My sister was horrified. 'You've destroyed its value,' she cried. 'It's not for sale,' I murmured.

Then there's my porcelain crèche. These figures look like they could be vintage Peter Jones, but I surround the willowy Mary, the courtly Joseph and the chunky baby Jesus with all of my Royal Copenhagen polar bears. It looks at home in the chalky blue drawing room.

But the crèche I love most is the one I bought last year from the Catholic Truth Society shop next to Westminster Cathedral. I used to visit this crèche before and after every RHS show at Vincent Square, and soon became friends with the young woman from Fife who runs the shop. Glynn told me about the monastic order of nuns in France

– the Sisters of Bethlehem – who create the figures out of a compound of granite and resin. In exotic language I didn't understand she explained that 'the nuns are not a Carthusian order but they have the same charism as St Bruno'. She showed me pictures of the monastery: pink buildings surrounded by vineyards.

I paid for the crèche in instalments, guiltily shuffling past the homeless who congregate in the piazza as I went in clutching my cheque book. I made my last payment as Advent began, and it took a trolley to wheel the boxes out to my car.

Each figure has the stillness and beauty of a Henry Moore sculpture. Mary's hands are outstretched so that she can hold her baby on her lap. Throughout the evening, I move him from lap to crib. When every figure is in place I light the candles. I think about the nun who sculpted the first figure, who lived in silence in her cell, an artist whose vocation was prayer. What she created reveals, preserves, delights. I hope someone told her.

December 2, 2004

II
Field Margins

BIRD BY BIRD

IN her book of 'Instructions on Writing and Life', Anne Lamott tells the story of her 10-year-old brother agonising over a book report on birds. He'd spent three months looking at birds, listening to bird song and learning their habits. The report was due the next day. He sat at the kitchen table, close to tears, surrounded by bird books, coloured pencils and paper, 'immobilised by the hugeness of the task ahead'. His father sat down beside him, put his arm around his shoulder and said: 'Bird by bird, buddy. Just take it bird by bird.'

Wise and helpful advice for the overwhelmed: start small. Ever since I read that passage, I've headed my lists of worries and chores 'Bird by bird', lists that are my ignition key. On Boxing Day evening my 'Bird by bird' began: Check the price of wheat.

It's not the random beginning you might think. In this part of the country, much depends on the price of wheat. Last January it was hovering round £112 per tonne. At harvest it fell to below £60. Who can run a business, make plans, organise life when the foundations are so unpredictable? Especially when the price of wheat halves and the price of fertiliser shoots up from £110 to £190 per tonne because of the increase in the price of oil. I never try to understand the crazy volatility of commodity prices that are influenced by droughts, floods, bumper crops, wipeouts, weak dollars, strong euros. I just try to figure out what we'll say to the bank manager when we meet in the new year.

I was just beginning to expand on my 'Bird by bird' when the news came on. Something serious but not about Iraq: a tsunami had devastated coasts on a map that looked like half the world. It was a word I'd never heard before but one that would become a part of the global vocabulary as the days passed and the numbers of dead and missing rose ever higher.

Even before the new year arrived, the price of wheat and fertiliser had lost its urgency. Other items on my list were also ignored. I didn't really need to order towels from the White Company, go to Waitrose, attend a dinner in London.

I grew up in the shadow of human defeat by a savage, unpredictable river: the Great Mississippi Flood of 1927, the greatest natural disaster America has known. The stories that gripped my heart as a child were never about princes and rabbits but tales of the carcasses of horses and cows floating past, of trains derailed and hanging in mid-air like twisted Gargantua, of the homes of nearly one million people erased from the land, of hundreds of thousands of black people driven north. Three decades on the tide marks were still pointed out to me, and stories of desperate attempts to establish order were as vivid as if I were there. I was mesmerised by the stained-glass window in a small church in the Delta: refugees huddled on the levee, terrified of the rising water below. 'And the rain descended, and the flood came, and the wind blew, and beat upon that house; and it fell, and great was the fall of it.' *Matthew 7:27.*

The '27 Flood marked my grandparents and, by the laws of inheritance, me. I inherited their belief that natural disasters re-shape society by reminding us, in the words of Paul Valéry, that 'civilisations are mortal'.

It's too soon to interpret this earthshaking tragedy, but in a time of uncertainty and anguish and despair there has been a surge of goodness and mercy. It's as though the world has found a portion of its lost heart. Maybe we can build on that. Bird by bird.

January 13, 2005

81

MUCH ADO

AS little girls, when we played weddings, Lee Case was always the bride because she was as skinny and graceful as a lovelorn Juliet, even at the age of five. Our groom was forced into the part by the female dictatorship that ruled the neighbourhood. When he died of meningitis aged 10, I spent the next 30 years wishing we had just once let Craig be the bride he so longed to be.

I was happy to be the preacher as long as I could dress as a nun. The bridesmaids wore lipstick and high heels and we solemnly hummed *Here Comes the Bride* as Lee glided down the driveway into the Church of the Garage. Hand on heart, I never wanted to be the bride. I never asked for a bride doll, and when I was confirmed aged 12 I did not see my white dress and headband as a dress rehearsal for my wedding. Which is just as well because I married 'late' – past 35 – which, where I come from, puts me right up there with the Romanian professor who has just begun motherhood.

Nowadays, marrying past one's virginal youth seems to cheer folks up. Three different friends sent me news about the December wedding at St Mark's Episcopal Church on Long Island of Freear Pollard and Robert Barnwell III, both from Greenwood, Mississippi. The bride, 62, and the bridegroom, 63, were childhood friends who met up again in New York last January. Part of their mutual attraction was just knowing each other's parents. The bride wore a cream silk satin gown with a long train, and her flower girls wore claret velvet. The reception in the parish hall had a large Christmas tree surrounded by bicycles, tricycles, Barbie dolls and inline skates. The merger of two mature households meant they had all the nice stuff they needed, so each guest was asked to bring a present for a needy child.

My bridegroom and I were not quite so philanthropic. We concentrated on the music and commissioned a song from the composer Nigel Hess whose music I had discovered at the Royal Shakespeare Company. We chose words from *Song of Solomon*, 'Rise up, my love and come away, for lo, the winter is past, the rain is over and gone', apt sentiments for late bloomers. Jill Gomez sang, and cousin Richard pronounced us man and wife. As we signed the register, the RSC choir sang spirituals – *Steal Away* and *Deep River*.

Last week we had one of those 'we are still married' celebrations: a concert at the Cadogan Hall off Sloane Square, formerly the Christian Science church and now the most beautiful and acoustically perfect concert hall in London. It was a glittering evening of Shakespearean music, verse and anecdote, narrated by Judi Dench and Patrick Stewart, and conducted by Mr Hess. Shakespeare inspired many English composers, but Mr Hess, as long-time composer for the RSC, has probably written more music for Shakespeare's plays than any other. Like a wedding, the concert was one of those 'once in a lifetime' evenings.

On the day I finally went down the aisle, I felt too old for a long train. Instead, dressed in palest pink Fortuny and leaning on my father's arm, I glided to the tinkling of bells and the haunting sound of a single cello. My English in-laws were mystified by the order of service – at the entrance of the bride, 'Overture to William Shakespeare's *Much Ado About Nothing*' by Mr Hess – but the bride and bridegroom thought it was perfect. Still, if we had it to do over again we would register our wedding list at Toys 'R' Us.

February 3, 2005

LOVE STORY

IT is the final day of pruning in the vineyard, and as I make my Thermos of coffee and search for secateurs I look longingly on the kitchen table at the morning papers. In font sizes usually reserved for natural disasters and war, the headlines beg me to sit and stay: 'The Long Love Story', 'The End of the Affair', 'Free at Last'. Maybe not as good as the *Bristol Evening Post*'s 'Tetbury Man to Wed', but I want to read every column inch. I put on my reading glasses to check out the engagement ring (is it sparkly enough for the bride-to-be to gaze at during the sermons, speeches and long banquets that await her?). I study the engaging, un-Botoxed wrinkles. A few more minutes and I could calculate the Body Mass Index of the future Duchess of Cornwall, a challenge that appeals to me more than pruning vines in the cold rain.

I cannot admit this to my husband, of course. In much the same way that Prince Charles finds contentment planting hellebores with Camilla, my husband likes me working alongside him in the vineyard. He likes me with my corduroy trousers tucked into my wellies, in the same way that I reckon Charles likes to see Camilla on a horse, hair tucked under her helmet. Country men have this hankering for country women.

Pruning is the foundation for all that a grape grower does for the rest of the year. Every act, every choice, builds on what is left on the mature vine after pruning. Over the years you learn that the cane closest to last year's now mature wood will be the most fruitful. The ideal pruner counts two buds up the root of that cane, allows a finger's width beyond and cuts. It is a blend of rote and concentration. There is contemplative comfort in the repetition, but you have to remember to stop every few vines to stretch your hands.

In this farming community that goes back to Domesday, nothing came so close to tearing it asunder as the rocky twilight of the marriage of Charles and Diana. The serialisation of Andrew Morton's book *Diana: Her True Story* led to our three-year boycott of *The Sunday Times*. After Charles's confessed adultery to Jonathan Dimbleby on television, we had enough strong feelings here to form two boxing teams. With Diana's 'three of us in this marriage' revelations on *Panorama*, we had to call for a moratorium on all things Windsor.

If I was worried that the announcement of the marriage would renew those deep divisions, a quick poll among the frosty vines revealed that feelings are not so strong. For a start, Camilla looks more 'first wife' than second. Many of the pruners – *femmes* of a certain age – have husbands the age of Prince Charles who have moved out (and in with 32-year-old lawyers/fund managers). The rant, 'What do these young women see in these 50-something men?', has become a chorus, but we know what the men see in the 32-year-olds. On this south-facing slope, Charles marrying Camilla feels like a victory for the qualities of warmth, humour, understanding and steadiness. The younger pruners, the ones who have grown up in the extended families of step-parents, have different feelings. They worry that the young princes won't be wild with joy. 'It takes a long time,' they say.

Pruning, like marriage, is an act of faith. When you decide what wood to cut away and what to leave behind, you don't know if there will be enough water to create juice or enough sun to create sweetness. But you have seen enough signs of hope to get on with it.

'Vines,' says my husband, 'are forgiving.'

'It's the beauty of mature wood,' I reply.

February 24, 2005

87

VIVE LA CHASSE

ON the day the fox-hunting ban came into law in England I left the country. It was not the revolutionary gesture once made by the likes of Wordsworth and Thomas Paine: my journey was to Nice via easyJet from Stansted to visit my Suffolk neighbour Jorn in his winter refuge on top of a Provençal hill. Still, I felt a certain lightness in my heart at being in the country with *les camarades* who had marched alongside us as we protested at the British government's aim to turn foxhunting into a class war and who have now opened their arms to the asylum-seekers from England's *chasseur de renards*.

Ah, the French. Who introduced England to the mounted hunt, a small detail lost in three centuries of hunting prints and tablemats. Who, in *esprit de contradiction*, smoke, drink and eat more fat than anyone in the world, yet have fewer heart problems and half the obesity rate of the British. Who work 35-hour weeks and take seven weeks of paid holidays a year, but are the fifth biggest economic power. Who are a proud republic but in the local *marchand de journaux* display six magazines with Charles and Camilla on the cover.

The south of France harbours no resentment towards the planeloads of British who arrive hourly on flights that cost less than steak frites at Café Rouge. Provence has always inspired outsiders – think Petrarch, Picasso, Peter Mayle. On my flight I sit next to two retired teachers from Lowestoft who found their house on the internet and now live in France permanently. They have a network of English friends including judges, doctors and bankers, and each morning they eat their croissants (80% fat) in their local café, and read their papers (both the *Daily Telegraph* and *The Times* are now printed in Marseilles). In the evenings they watch BBC1 and BBC2 on their French television.

France is the same size as Texas, and the vast majority of its citizens live in cities, but with every bite of Brie or Roquefort they experience an agricultural sense of place. When French farmers block the Champs-Elysées they have wide public understanding that comes from a national love of *terroir*, a more soulful word than 'land'. The French believe that *la chasse* – be it foxes, wild boar or partridges – is part of their common heritage.

My French friends are mystified by the English. They maintain that they love Ellen MacArthur more than the English – who are too '*fixés*' on the technical assistance she had, not on her phenomenal strength and courage. '*Quelle cynisme,*' cries Antoine, '*elle est formidable!*' He expresses moral indignation at the cynicism of the *urbaniste* government of Monsieur Blair, who went to war after 41 hours of debate on Iraq in the House of Commons but gave 275 hours to the debate on foxhunting. '*Imbécile!*'

Jorn and I dwell on these cultural issues as we drink our Bandol (14.2 degrees alcohol) in the local restaurant in Valbonne that has just reopened after a four-week *congé annuel.* Ar the table behind us a party of six smokes *avant* and *après* their foie gras. Across from us, a couple dine with their cocker spaniel, who has its own chair and cushion. Dogs and smoking are banned in French restaurants, but no one heeds, or enforces, these laws.

But the message is clear: if we want to live the long and happy lives of the French, we must not slavishly obey laws that are *défavorable.* What we anxiouslv call civil disobedience, the French call *savoir faire.* Vive la France!

March 3, 2005

THE EASTER VIGIL

ON the day of his exams, my friend Nicholas's mother would pat him on the back and say, 'Remember, darling, 70% is just as good as 100%.' When Nicholas presented her with his reports, she would tell him, 'But, sweetheart, I'm not interested in marks: what have you *learned*?'

This is the mother I want to be. This is the mother I am not. Instead I nag, nag, nag. I have bought into the conspiracy theory that the GCSEs Sam faces this spring will determine the universities he applies to two years down the road. That the university he goes to will determine his career choices. That the career choices will determine all future happiness in life.

'I hate Lent,' wrote Jonathan Swift, in 1712. He hated the 'sour, devout faces of People who only put on Religion for seven weeks'. I worry that someday Sam will say, 'I hate Easter', because its spiritual resonance will be forever blurred by memories of revising for exams. His Easter vigil is not the Vision but the Revision: Common Entrance,

GCSEs, AS levels, A levels. Will he remember the happy chaos of dyeing eggs, the rainy egg hunts, the tonnes of Cadbury mini eggs, the egg tree with its hand-painted Russian eggs dangling on screwy twigs of hazel 'Contorta'? Will he have good memories of the glorious services in the cathedral, of a happy gang of family and friends lingering over delicious meals at a dining table covered in moss and eggs, of the passionate games of Articulate, Trivial Pursuit and pots of mint tea in the drawing room? Or will he remember only that as the last guest departed on Easter Monday the cramming regime began. Latin. Chemistry. Biology. Maths. French. Classical Civilisation.

Only his beloved dog, Bofus, loyally camped at his feet, penetrates the enforced solitude of the study chamber. The playwright John Osborne believed that a dog was a child's best teacher, providing a perfect form of moral and emotional instruction. A dog initiates him into containing the power of the pack, the needs of those who demand you to lead as well as love them. He believed that dogs instil more practical wisdom about selflessness, procreation and death than schools or even parents.

Osborne also liked to tell how the first few bars of the *Enigma Variations* were inspired by Elgar's great bulldog, Dan, falling down a steep bank of the River Wye, then paddling upstream in search of a landing place (bars two and three) and his rejoicing bark on reaching dry land (second half of bar five). The organist at Hereford

Cathedral suggested that the composer set it to music. 'And I did,' wrote Elgar. In the autograph draft of *Variations*, he inscribed just one word: 'Dan.'

In fact, Elgar is as good a reason as any to lighten up, to surrender Sam's education to Bofus. The greatest musician England has produced for 300 years, Elgar attended neither public school nor university and had no formal musical training. Away from the treadmill of academic strictures and exams, the composer was free to find his own path.

These are my thoughts as I melt down a large Green and Black's chocolate egg, slowly whisking in the Jersey milk to make a sumptuous cup of hot chocolate, a gesture of encouragement for Sam whose head is barely visible behind the files of revision papers. I silently vow to tell him that success, like happiness, is best pursued obliquely. That marks really don't matter; it's what you learn. As I hand him the rich, steamy offering, the words come tumbling out of my mouth: 'If you don't get all As in your GCSEs you will die poor and lonely.'

April 7, 2005

THE NIGHTINGALE PROPHECY

A FEW weeks ago, I sat listening to *Charlotte's Web* on the radio. The house was full of children but I couldn't tether any of them to a kitchen chair. The 16-year-old rolls his eyes heavenward and goes back to *The Da Vinci Code*. Even Miles, aged nine, is glued to Anthony Horowitz. Not for them the story of a large, grey spider called Charlotte, 'about the size of a gumdrop', and a spring pig with a sweet nature, called Wilbur.

Most of *Charlotte's Web* takes place in the Zuckerman barn, through the passing of the four seasons:

'Life in the barn was very good – night and day, winter and summer, spring and fall, dull days and bright days. It was the best place to be...with the garrulous geese, the changing seasons, the heat of the sun, the passage of swallows, the nearness of rats, the sameness of sheep, the love of spiders, the smell of manure, and the glory of everything.'

I've been thinking about the Zuckerman farm all week as I watched lambs play tag in Kitchen Meadow, listened to the peacock and guinea fowl chorus, and succumbed to the tenderness and humour of my Call ducks. The glory of everything.

Almost everything. This morning I buried Brother, my bashful Buff Orpington cockerel, decapitated at dawn by a fox. His death was my fault. Shutting up the hens last night I suddenly heard a nightingale and sank into the sweet-smelling straw of the chicken house. When the concert ended I forgot to cross the yard to shut the door in Brother's solitary sleeping quarters. He never had a chance.

It was as much the timing as the beauty of the nightingale's song that distracted me. I don't remember ever hearing this creature so early. But, then, everything is early now: cherry blossom, daffodils, wheat, barley, the dawn chorus.

It's what happens when, according to Sir David King, Britain's most senior scientist, the 10 hottest years on record have occurred since 1990, including the past five. Sir David warns that it may be too late to reverse the effects of global warming. Even the Pentagon is alarmed about the melt of the Arctic that seems to be releasing so much fresh water into the North Atlantic. They know that a weakening Gulf Stream could yield abrupt and overwhelming change, the kind of climate change that would make the policy battles over education, pensions, hospitals and tax futile. But there is something cynical about politicians who say that climate change is the most serious problem facing the world today and have no policy, no vision, no commitment to tackle it.

Charlotte's Web is a book about trust and treachery, adventure and miracle, life and death, the seasons – and a spider who cannot stand hysterics: 'Slowly, slowly,' says Charlotte. 'Never hurry, and never worry.' Our relationship with planet Earth has been one of trust and treachery, life and death, the seasons, but if we are going to save our planet we must worry, we must hurry.

Charlotte saves Wilbur because she can write – can and does. 'It is not often that someone comes along who is a true friend and a good writer. Charlotte was both.' Maybe it's stretching it to see E. B. White's book as a mission statement, a prophetic tale for our time, but it's more convincing than the party manifestos. I've now had a look at all three. Frankly, I couldn't call any of the party leaders persuasive writers or true friends of the Earth. My vote will go to the heroine who writes 'Earth First' in her web.

April 28, 2005

PAYING THE PRICE

MY friend Rose calls from Virginia to tell me a southern belle story. A Spartanburg lady was driving to a cocktail party when she had a flat tyre. She got out of her car and waved down the first trucker who drove by.

'A trucker!' her friends exclaim in horror. 'Good heavens, you could have been raped!'

'Well, I thought about that,' she says. 'But I reckon I can muddle my way through a rape, and I don't know a damn thing about changing a tyre.'

Rose has southern belle pedigree, including a degree from a college called Sweetbriar. She's also a lawyer who defends folks who wouldn't stick out in a Faulkner novel, and she can change a tyre wearing sling-backs and a Chanel suit (size 4). I met her in the Seventies when she lived in London. Like all Virginians, she is Anglophile to the bone.

'I'm never coming to England again,' she says on the telephone.

'What do you mean?'

'Do you know what the exchange rate is?!' she snarls in her Virginia accent.

I do. It's nearly two dollars to the pound. Americans who used to come to England every year are now staying home, muttering about a president who's 'gonna bankrupt the country'. These are Americans who love English cathedrals and West End plays, Heywood Hill bookshop and Tate Britain, the Chelsea Flower Show and Great Dixter.

But there's another group of Americans over here who can't stay home because Starbucks reaches five bucks: the thousands of Americans stationed on airbases throughout Britain.

Over the years I've got to know some of these Americans, who rent two of our cottages. Lakenheath and Mildenhall, the two largest American airbases in Europe, are 25 minutes from here and our tenants are usually pilots and their families. We try to look after the wives and children left on their own while husbands are in Afghanistan and Iraq. We celebrate their homecomings.

When Sam was small, they'd take him along to the air fête at RAF Mildenhall, an annual event that brought out half-a-million people to watch the planes. He loved the base's Disney-like world of Main Street America: Dunkin' Donuts, Taco Bell, Popeye's Chicken. But all that ended after September 11. Security tightened. The air fête was cancelled. This year is the first since 2001 that a fête, albeit with 'static aircraft', is scheduled. That is, *was* scheduled. Now it's been cancelled. New terrorist threats? No, it's a bigger problem: a $3 billion budget deficit in the air force.

'The exchange rate is a killer,' explains Roy, who flies helicopters. 'But this is about the war in Iraq.' They've also axed the shuttle buses and cable TV on base. He gives me a polite smile, but I see the worry in his face.

The adrenaline that flows in the early days of war doesn't look at price tags. I doubt that when the war in Iraq started, Bush or Blair or Brown had any idea what it would ultimately cost.

I reckon the American bases in England will shrink even further. Families will be left behind in Florida and Oklahoma. And America and England will start to leave Iraq. Not because the war is won or because the body bags are too painful – neither Bush nor Blair has ever attended a funeral of a soldier killed in Iraq – but because they can't pay the bills. You can muddle through a lot of things, but you can't muddle through a war.

May 12, 2005

READ ALL ABOUT IT

AH, the joy of country life. Cockerels crowing, sheep baaing, ducks nesting, wheat growing. It's much nicer than *The Archers* would have you believe, and some days it almost seems like a peaceable kingdom. But there is one aspect of city and suburban life that I hanker after: newspapers delivered to the doorstep at the crack of dawn.

If you live outside a village nowadays you might as well live in Timbuktu. Freckle-faced boys on bicycles delivering papers before school are a thing of the past. Even their replacement, sleepy mothers in dressing gowns, driving their sons along their paper rounds, have disappeared. Maybe mothers all have full-time jobs now and provide their 12-year-olds with generous pocket money, but if you want an early-morning paper in the country you have to drive to the village.

Getting dressed and driving to collect the paper seriously punctures the pleasure of sitting with a cup of coffee and editing the world at the kitchen table. Still, once the papers are in front of you, you are in control. Skim the news about who's who in the cabinet, read Simon Jenkins's column. Study carefully the ideal breakfast on the GI diet: the day is so much more digestible with a morning newspaper.

But in the category of 'America today, Britain tomorrow' (think hypochondria, litigation, the mall), newspapers over there are suffering from their sharpest decline in circulation history. Some of the blame falls on television news and internet sites, and most newspapers have free (for now) online sites offering much of what is in the printed paper. Under-25s rely almost entirely on the internet (my 24-year-old nephew calls newspapers the voice of middle age) and news that arrives via text message.

The sharpest fall is in the gargantuan Sunday papers, which is understandable. The Saturday papers are more manageable and more reliable, spread out over a weekend, and take up less space in the recycling bin. From time to time we decide to stop getting the Sunday papers and feel intellectually and ecologically virtuous. Then we creep back into the habit, usually after spending a weekend in a house that has five Sunday papers on the sideboard in the dining room, along with cooked breakfasts, a style of life that Sam yearns for us to emulate.

When I visit friends who don't read newspapers I find myself becoming irritable. It's as though we don't speak the same language or share a common culture. I even get cranky when my friends (more and more) say they prefer reading *The New York Times* online, relieved of the hassle of recycling the papers. 'But you can't distill the news looking at a screen; you can't feel the enjoyment, can't tear out the article and stick it on the fridge. You don't linger the same way, study the photographs, smell the ink!' I rant but I do not convert.

I know it would be wise to prepare myself for a world in which newspapers will become a piece of nostalgia, like glass milk-bottles, naps and radios with dials. Civilisation moves on, ever less civilised. But when the newspapers are a relic of the past I'm damned if I know what we'll use to stuff in our wet shoes to keep their shape, line the floor of the chicken house, keep out the draughts in the lambing sheds, and house-train puppies.

May 19, 2005

CATHEDRALIST AT THE SHOWDOWN

ALTHOUGH I'm converted to the belief that clearing clutter can radically transform your life, my house offers scant proof. Like Christian Scientists who re-read the writings of Mary Baker Eddy to keep themselves invigorated and true, I study *Clear Your Clutter* every six months just to find a surface.

Paper clutter is condemned utterly, and I've religiously tossed out magazines, newspapers, wedding invitations and school reports. So it's amazing that the Order of Service for the Installation of the 81st Dean of Lincoln Cathedral, May 12, 1989, has survived. That ceremony ignited a period of intense turbulence: a zealous and fiery dean in battle with a liberal and dogged sub-dean. Minster Yard became a battlefield of pious hatred that even Trollope could not have envisioned. My only reason for keeping this record is the inscription inside to Saint Hugh, who rebuilt the cathedral after the earthquake in 1185. It begins:

Hugh
Trained to not feel cold & hunger
To see the King in the Beggar
To see the Beggar in the King...
To laugh spiritual laughter...
To call the bluff of false reverence...
To reconcile with ready wit...
To be cool at a showdown &
At the showdown of death to see Heaven.

It's longer than that, and I've never tracked down who wrote it, but my periodic reunions with St Hugh meant that when I received my invitation to the Installation and Seating of the Reverend Doctor Samuel Thames Lloyd III as ninth dean of the National Cathedral in Washington, I wasn't thrown by the word 'Installation', merely wary. I couldn't shake off the memory of huge and sad divisions that I associate with the dean's job.

Sam Lloyd, husband of my beloved cousin Marguerite, is an unusual man of God for these times. With a PhD in English literature (he wrote his doctoral thesis on the poetry of Robert Penn Warren), he brings literary order and grace to his sermons. Perhaps it's his love of literature – as well as living with two teenagers, daughter Cooper, 17, and son Gabriel, 15 – but Sam, to a rare degree, lives a complete and rounded existence, all the better for healing divisions.

And the Installation a few weeks ago in that magnificent

and youngest of cathedrals was grand and beautiful. As Sam wryly put it: 'Welcome to the world of cathedrals...which by nature do things grandly and beautifully, offering an experience of God and the things of God that stretch our imaginations and beggar our words.'

Not a lover of pomp and ceremony, Sam believes the National Cathedral, where presidents are regularly blessed and occasionally mourned, is called to be a place of reconciliation. Washington is now more divided – economically, racially and politically – than ever. The Episcopal Church is also painfully fractured.

The cathedralist in me sat in a stained-glass trance, filled with a sense of sacred space. The secular me chewed over a *Harper's* article I'd read on the plane: 30 million members of the Association of Evangelicals, one quarter of America's eligible voters, were all urged (strongly) to vote for Bush.

With perfect clarity and poetry, Sam calls for a generous-spirited Christianity, the cathedral as a place of reconciliation and healing. Listening to this cousin-by-marriage makes me feel like a member of the wedding. I'm not sure I'll make it down the aisle of forgiveness – the power of the fundamentalists and evangelicals scares me stiff – but I understand what the new Dean is saying: we must clear our clutter and make room in our minds for one another.

May 26, 2005

HANGING ON TO AWE

TWO weeks after I started first grade, a six-year-old boy was kidnapped in Kansas City, Missouri, by a woman who came to his school claiming to be the boy's aunt. The Bobby Greenlease kidnapping case was almost as famous as the Lindbergh baby case in the Thirties, and I pushed my fledgling reading skills up a few levels in order to read the gruesome daily accounts in the local paper. This was in that once-upon-a-time when parents hid bad news from their children, so I felt it was my job to warn my fellow six-year-olds about strangers posing as relatives. Each morning at recess, as we gathered round the swings, I told the latest instalment. We all cried when the little boy's body was found, and we hollered when the kidnappers were caught. Then parents complained and I was kept in at recess with a stack of Easy Readers. I never did get to tell the bit about the electric chair.

However, through no fault of my own, the smoky fire of nervous melancholy was laid. Here's the formula: happy excitement – new school, new shoes, new dress – and then, a thousand miles away, another six-year-old is kidnapped. Give me a happy occasion and I'm instantly on the lookout for the little patch of heartbreak lurking round the corner, a small nub of unease to chew away at. This week it was Chelsea. Truly, nothing fertilises my fear and sorrow like the glorious Chelsea Flower Show.

On the Monday, Chelsea is like the opening night of an opera on a biblical scale. In less than three weeks, wildflower meadows, slender canals, tunnels of weeping hornbeams and prairies of miscanthus grass have been created, a miracle of human endeavour, nature, luck, genius and adrenaline. Every *Iris sibirica* opens, 50ft bamboos take root, and the vital hard stuff – slate from Lancashire, granite from Africa, pebbles from India – slots in place. Fountains gently gurgle in this self-contained five-day cameo state of grace.

And so my anxiety begins. I flinch as I hear the waspish comments of amateur judges searching for defects. (The real judges, all 122 of them, are tight-lipped.) I cringe at the quick gazes that pass on in search of something even more amazing/stunning/perfect. I ache for the tired designers, craftsmen, nurserymen and gardeners required to distil their long labour into the briefest soundbite. My tour of the gardens becomes less an Ode to Joy, more a Lamentation for the Loss of Our Sense of Awe.

Then, nestled in its corner site, the requisite 230 sq m,

another world: a slightly unkempt village green; a fuzzy, neglected pond; a human-sized pub; a vegetable patch – 'A Soldier's Dream of Blighty', the dream that kept the British soldiers going during the Second World War. Two Chelsea Pensioners, retired soldiers who fought in that war, sit in the garden enjoying a pint in the shifting light and shade. And then the uneasy melancholy begins to swell. What does today's soldier dream of Blighty? Will the judges, unsentimental professionals, think this is horticultural nostalgia? I gaze at the vegetable patch, its pre-war cultivars grown entirely by the Chelsea Pensioners, working from a 1939 Suttons seed catalogue, and I hope for the best.

At 7am on Tuesday the award cards are delivered to the gardens. The Chelsea Pensioners' Garden gets Gold and Best in Show. My relief is huge, but it quickly hits a snag: If only this little patch of Chelsea could remain, a safe and shady corner for these lovely men in their red coats, a souvenir of an unclouded vision of Britain as the peace is celebrated.

June 2, 2005

BENDING TOWARDS JUSTICE

MY grandfather, prosecuting attorney in a small Mississippi hill town for more than 40 years, believed that a nation's concept of justice to the individual is at the heart of its civilisation. A county prosecutor who opposed the death penalty and a member of the Mississippi legislature who doubted the Resurrection, he fought all his life against a judicial system with the capacity to be vindictive, unjust, pitiless or vengeful. Over the years this man, who wore seersucker suits from April until October, has grown in my memory to be morally as tall as Atticus in *To Kill a Mockingbird*.

Watching the prosecuting attorney in the Michael Jackson trial made me think about my grandfather. Maybe it is grafting hopeful thinking on to sepia memory, but I reckon Papa would never have allowed that case to go to court. I wonder what he would have made of another trial, less than 40 miles from his legal patch. The first I heard about it was Friday evening in the kitchen, listening to *PM* on Radio

4 as I trimmed my last asparagus of the season. It was the final news slot, and I lifted my head when I heard the words 'Mississippi' and '41 years later, a murder trial', the names 'Chaney, Schwerner and Goodman'. In the coolness of an English summer evening I sat down and wept.

The tragic journey of the three young civil rights workers – two white men from the north, one black man from Mississippi – into the heart of Klan country on Sunday, June 21, 1964, to investigate the burning of the black Mount Zion Methodist Church is now a part of American history. The details are familiar from the film *Mississippi Burning*: how they were arrested at 3pm by a deputy sheriff on the outskirts of Philadelphia, Mississippi, kept in jail until 10.30 that night, released and stopped again 10 miles outside of town; the gangland-style killing by Klansmen; their burial in a dam under construction in a remote area of the county. By the time the FBI found their bodies 44 days later my own family had watched a cross burn in our front yard, lived under a siege of bomb threats. The crime? To try and penetrate the frozen world of fear and violence.

What *Mississippi Burning* failed to show was that no one was ever tried for the murders. In 1967 the federal government returned 19 indictments for 'conspiracy to violate the civil rights' of the three dead men. Witnesses said that Klan leader Edgar Ray Killen wasn't present at the killings, but Preacher Killen was the mastermind who summoned the Klansmen and chose the killing and burial sites. Eleven members of the jury wanted to convict him, but one held out – a woman who could 'never convict a preacher'.

This trial will be one of the last of the South's 'atonement trials', with a new generation of jurors and prosecutors snatching the old dragons from their air-conditioned pick-ups and putting them where they belong. In 1994 Byron de la Beckwith was convicted of the 1963 murder of civil rights activist Medgar Evers. Three years ago, Bobby Frank Cherry was convicted of the 1963 bombing of a Birmingham church that killed four black girls.

Folks will always say that 40 years have passed. Let old men die in their own beds. But I inherited prosecutor's genes. I believe that murder is murder. It's never too late for justice.

June 23, 2005

111

THE GOOD GOOD-BYE

'HENRY Lyulph Holland, 1st Earl of Shane, had existed for so long that the public had begun to regard him as immortal. The public, as a whole, finds reassurance in longevity: the long-liver has triumphed over at least one of man's initial handicaps – the brevity of life.'

The opening lines of Vita Sackville-West's novel *All Passion Spent* pull me right back into my Hogarth Press edition. When I first read it 30 years ago, some passages were lost on me: 'Earl of Shane, KG, GCB, GCSI, GCIE, etc etc. – his diminishing honours trailing away behind him like the tail of a comet', but I understood 88-year-old Lady Shane who, after seven decades devoted to the demands of her husband and children, finally, in her widowhood, chooses to live independently in a tiny house in Hampstead.

Years later, I learned from Victoria Glendinning's biography that it was Vita's mother-in-law, Lady Carnock, who gave her the idea for the novel. Lady Carnock had clung tenaciously to the family home; Lady Shane in the novel does what Vita thought Lady Carnock ought to have done.

Back then I didn't understand the tribal procedure of aristocratic primogeniture. I was more familiar with ordinary mortals who create a home and garden that they occupy for life, but literature and history led me to the world of the nobility and demi-nobility who are merely the stewards of their great houses. When the sons inherit, mothers must move on, sometimes into the dower house a discreet distance from the main house, sometimes into a cottage converted to her taste, occasionally to a modest flat near Peter Jones.

At first these evictions seemed heartless to me, but I've now lived long enough to witness close up widows who have resisted all the machinery of the siege that emotion can bring to bear, refusing to be dislodged even when their own children and grandchildren are living in cramped keeper's cottages. These women wander in solitary splendour through a Christo-like universe of acres of dust-sheets, imposing an out-of-date formality on daughters-in-law and grandchildren. By clinging on, they are saying: 'I am more important than the history of this place and its future', thus depriving the estate of the sunlight, oxygen, fun and rigorous energy (economic and emotional) needed to keep old houses alive. With agricultural income on the wane, estates have had to reinvent themselves; but the effort needed to produce income – to create music festivals, literary festivals, farm shops, gift shops, garden festivals – is huge and barely makes a dent when it comes to reroofing and rewiring.

Because these things are so hard to say ('Mummy, have you ever thought...'), maybe what's needed is a slender volume the size of a prayer book. It could be called *The Good Good-bye*, with chapters on when and how to move out, preferably not at knifepoint. The first chapter should be on the pleasure of choosing and renovating the dower house before you are dowered, and the freedom to take only the most cherished possessions: the best furniture, one set of favourite china, the most-loved paintings, editing life so that everything is distilled to its essence, moving from quantity to quality. Until this book appears, you'll have to go to Heywood Hill for a copy of *All Passion Spent*. Its fierce simplicities still have the power to inspire. Read it, then send your copy to whom it may concern.

July 7, 2005

LIFELINE OF THE COUNTRYSIDE

IT'S not the kind of milestone that usually gets acknowledged: Sam in London on his own. While his father is judging water gardens at Hampton Court, Sam has the city at his feet. He takes his Sage fishing rod to Farlows for a repair, then takes the tube to a magic shop in Camden Town to add to his magic and juggling kit. He takes two more tube journeys to arrange his work experience – a week in July with Citigroup Venture Capital, a week in August with the lawyer Tim Lawson-Cruttenden – before meeting up with his friend Harry who's doing his work experience at the *Daily Mail*. They go for lunch at an Italian restaurant: 16-year-olds going on 25. Then he takes the tube to Liverpool Street and a train home. A happy day. An independent day. The day before the bombs exploded in that crescent of London that is the first port of call for country dwellers on this side of England.

I am more shaken by last week's bombs than Sam. I keep

thinking: what if he had been there. *Without me*. And Sam is still excited about his two weeks in London this summer, even though his real love is country life. Before he was three he could tell wheat from barley and identify every make of tractor. Other milestones: his first 4.10 (followed by his first rabbit, squirrel, pheasant, grouse). His first fishing rod, first brown trout, rainbow trout and, last summer, two salmon on the Halladale. The countryside, its fields, rivers and pleasures, are bred in his bone. But something else has been imbued in him from an early age: you can't make a living here. Doctor, lawyer, banker – actually, the choices aren't as many as they once seemed: you need a career that will produce the income that will sustain the farm you love. That translates: work in London.

In fact, we didn't need to drum this into his head. When he was at prep school near Ipswich, his friends lived in old rectories and sprawling farmhouses in Essex, Suffolk and Norfolk: all within viable reach of a train to Liverpool Street station. The fathers (and a few mothers) got up at the crack of dawn to be in the City or Gray's Inn by 8am. Even the fathers with large farming estates, such as Freddie Clarke's father, Duncan, put in years in the City in order to bankroll the diversification projects that just might make the land pay. This is the country life of the 21st century, where the car parks surrounding the Victorian train stations are bigger than wheat fields, and advertisements for country houses include a crucial detail:

London Liverpool Street, 65 minutes; King's Cross, 45 minutes. London is the lifeline of the countryside.

The first time I appeared on this page – March 7, 1996 – I wrote about booking tickets to *Starlight Express* during the days of IRA bombings. 'The trip to London is the country child's half-term treat. Before we leave I write on six strips of paper, "My name is Sam Carlisle. I am seven years old and I am with my mother. In case of emergency please telephone...", and stuff them into his trouser pockets, jacket pockets, shirt pockets. I put one in my coat pocket as well and cross my fingers.'

The days of stuffing pockets are over. The first interview I heard on the radio after the explosions was that of a 16-year-old from Deal in Kent, in London for his work experience – 'There was a bang. The lights went out. I thought I was dead.' Next week Sam will be a 16-year-old working in London. Call it stage one of the job he'll have in order to be able to afford the privilege of living in the country. My fingers are crossed.

July 14, 2005

ARE WE NEARLY THERE?

THE hall is filled with fishing rods, golf clubs, wellies and duffle bags on wheels stuffed with each person's idea of the essentials for a week in Scotland. The earthquake of departure is nearly over, and what hasn't been done by now will have to wait.

The dogs lie low, and I don't have the heart to tell them that they are staying home. A keeper once told me that dogs don't have a sense of time: a week is the same as a day. Still, it's reassuring to think that the canine clock doesn't know the difference between a trip to Waitrose and a week in Perthshire. Which doesn't mean dogs are dumb, merely philosophical, like children sent away to boarding school.

Everyone else is asleep, and I go from room to room saying goodbye, just as I went round the garden this evening bidding farewell to late roses. I apologised to the kitchen garden for leaving just as it begins to shine. I picked all the broad beans for our supper so that we won't have to eat the tough big toes they'll turn into during our absence.

The truth is, I think that summer is the time for staying home. The water in the lake is warm enough to swim in every day now, sweet peas are in flower and the raspberries are at their peak. I have my morning coffee in the apple orchard with the chickens, and every evening we eat dinner in the garden. We wait all year for this moment. Like a snail being pushed off its rock, I wonder: why are we leaving?

You could say that Scotland is a compromise: a common language, no messy money, rivers, hills and no air miles. We cram the moulded Halford's cockroach on top of the car with all the outsize gear, leave an hour later than planned and hope to get to the farm café on the other side of Scotch Corner for breakfast outside with all our egos safely intact. The next stop is John Norris in Penrith, a concession to Sam who gazes at reels and flies with the same concentration that I bring to Georg Jensen jewellery on eBay. The only difference is that I have more buying power, a glaring injustice that feels more obvious on holidays. By the time we reach Dunkeld and the River Tay, the urge for reckless consumption will be replaced by the simple desire to fish.

And that is what the holidays are about. This is your inheritance, we say without saying: memories of summer and family. I have friends who are sane, intelligent people, who spend their lives planning holidays – and there are so many days to fill: half-terms, Christmas, Easter, two months in summer, each break an investment in the trust fund of memory.

I would like to pass on a different legacy: that you never have to be ashamed of staying put. That the world is wide but you don't have to see it all at once. You don't even have to see it all. That people are more interesting than places, and mileage is no guarantee of excitement. I tell Sam that Beethoven never went far but left immortal travel notes: a 10-mile journey to Baden gave mankind his Ninth Symphony. 'How random is that?' he replies.

The confined space of the Peugeot 407 requires tact and tolerance. As soon as we see Scottish hills my heart will melt like ice cream in the sun. I know if Sam catches a salmon his joy will sustain him throughout the year. As we head north Michael Morpurgo is on the radio, filling in for Mark Tully in *Something Understood*. 'Home is not where you belong,' he says. 'It's where you are.'

July 28, 2005

SEEING IS BELIEVING

MY capacity for being 'born again' has dwindled with the music of time. When I went forward to be 'saved' at the summer tent revivals that were our only pastime on hot summer evenings, my sister claimed I was 'just showin' off'. I was also collecting the modest loot given to the newly converted: pencils printed with 'Jesus Saves' in gold letters, and small metal crosses too flimsy to see you through an active Christian day. Not that I would have worn them. My family were Episcopalians who did not believe in religious display. Although I was fascinated by Southern Baptists who were baptised in the Tallahatchie River, and mesmerised by the Pentecostals who handled snakes and spoke in tongues, I was brought up in the discreet, zeal-free faith of the Anglican church.

We weren't just Anglicans. We were high Anglicans. Father Chrysler chanted services in plainsong. Incense stung our eyes on holy days, and we wore sooty dots on our foreheads on Ash Wednesday. The blood of Jesus

Christ was real wine from a silver chalice, and we felt spiritually superior to the Methodists who drank grape juice from Dixie cups.

Except for *The Church is One Foundation* and some Easter hymns and Christmas carols, the musical side of our worship was not convincing. Thanks to the Baptists, I can sing every verse of *I Was Sinking Deep with Sin* and *The Old Rugged Cross*, but Anglican hymns are as tricky as T. S. Eliot set to music by Benjamin Britten: not easily engraved in tuneful memory.

Sometimes I miss the spiritual lustiness of those summer evenings long ago. In a vague way, I'm always on the spiritual lookout. I read Ronald Blythe, who carries me through the seasons and the liturgy from harvest to harvest. When 'Thought for the Day' comes on, I flip off the kettle and listen, just in case the 'Thought' clears my spiritual fog. And for the past six years I've watched a miracle taking place here in my market town of Bury St Edmunds: the creation of a cathedral tower.

I don't use the word 'miracle' easily. How this tower got built – how it found acceptance from the existentialist Millennium Commission, how it combined the inspiration and legacy of the cathedral architect Stephen Dykes Bower, who left £2.4 million for the 'completion of the cathedral', including his plan for a spire, and then how Dykes Bower's assistant of 30 years, the architect Hugh Mathew, produced a more distinguished, more glorious design – it is all miraculous stuff. Even the Barnack stone from a quarry exhausted in 1450 by the building of Ely and Peterborough Cathedrals was discovered to have a rich seam. More than 8,000 tonnes were extracted to provide the 2,000 tonnes of the very best stone in England. A miracle as good as those loaves and fishes.

Carved stone was laid upon carved stone. Flints were knapped, lime mortar mixed. It has taken a mere six years to build a 150 ft perpendicular Gothic tower that will last another 1,000 years. And the tower has already begun to assert its spiritual authority. Whether you are on Angel Hill or in the Waitrose car park, you look up and are astonished. I'm not saying that the tower rids all doubt – this is not the Age of Faith – but it quickens the spirit. Emily Dickinson wrote: 'We believe and disbelieve a hundred times an Hour, which keeps Believing nimble.' The majestic Cathedral Tower, a sacred silhouette in the secular prairie of Suffolk sky, makes Believing nimble. It feels like a miracle.

August 4, 2005

LIVES AND LETTERS

'WHEN my mother died, she left me a bookstore. In England, you would call it a bookshop, but I prefer the word store. It suggests a treasure house to me, a place full of riches and surprises.'

So begins Joanna Trollope's short story 'Faith' about three people and their dreams. It's as perfect as Chekhov, and those five clean words are as evocative as any in literature: '...she left me a bookstore.'

My own bookstore dream was set in Paris: a shop in the Palais Royale. The gloomy *antiquaire* – a specialist in military medals and lead soldiers – was retiring after 30 years to his family home in Normandy. The shop was small but beautiful, with French grey walls and a circular staircase that led to an upstairs room, complete with a corner *cuisine* and a small loo.

My dream was to open an English bookshop called 'Lives and Letters'. Leatherbound memoirs would line the walls, and Chesterfield sofas and refectory tables would furnish the room. At twilight I would pull the curtains and the shop would become my sitting room. Upstairs my single *lit-bateau* would occupy a corner of the office, complete with the computer needed for an efficient mail-order service. This was a good decade before Amazon and AbeBooks, but my friend David at Faber and Faber assured me that mail order was the future.

There were a few hiccups in my 'Lives and Letters' dream. For a start, I had never sold a book in my life. Indeed, I did not own a computer and, moreover, I had no money beyond what I earned teaching English. Although I possessed a *carte de travaille*, a French driving licence and paid French taxes, I was still a foreigner. No small drawback. The fatal obstacle, however, was the elaborate lease, a relic of the Napoleonic code: the *entreprise commerciale* could not be a *domicile*. I could nap there after *déjeuner* but I could not crawl into bed after my *dîner*. I contemplated ignoring this ancient law but began having nightmares about blackout curtains and an Anne Frank existence, trembling as I silently brushed my teeth in darkness. Even in my most optimistic moments I knew it would be folly to embark on an adventure that required two monthly rent payments and uncertain revenue.

Whenever I walk into a perfect bookshop the dream comes back to me. It happened again this week in Scotland. Members of our house party had discovered a 'wonderful new bookshop in Aberfeldy'. While everyone else planned how many Munros they could climb in five days, I plotted my trip to Aberfeldy.

The Watermill bookshop is located in a Grade A-listed stone mill. The miller's widow turned down countless offers to develop it into housing, but when two Londoners who had recently moved to Perthshire, Jayne and Kevin Ramage, approached her with their dream to create a bookshop and art gallery, she softened: at least the mill would still be a part of the community.

And it is a dream bookshop, a treasure house of riches and surprises. The mill generates electricity for the building. Old library trolleys are fitted with industrial wheels. There's a reading room, a café, a terrace outside and a gallery on the top floor. As Colette (legally domiciled above a shop in the Palais Royale) would have described it: peaceful and exciting.

It took two years to convert the mill from oats to books, but in less than two months The Watermill has achieved what devolution and politicians can only dream of: a haven for lovers of the printed word.

August 11, 2005

THE PUSH OF TIME

I GREW up in the days when grown-ups still talked about where they were when they heard about Pearl Harbor. I knew by heart the story of how my mother heard the news that Sunday morning on the car radio driving back from a dance in Memphis, how all the young men at the dance enlisted the day after December 7, 1941.

The magnetic timeline for my generation began the day Kennedy was shot. My son knows how I wandered out of school that Friday in a shocked daze and walked home, a truancy that became a permanent part of my school records: *November 22, 1963, absent without permission.* We tell these stories to keep alive our memories, as a kind of *memento mori* tangled up in the unconscious mantra of 'never again'.

Then came September 11, 2001, telegraphed into our collective consciousness as 9/11. Now more people are alive who witnessed the crumbling of the Twin Towers on their television screens than have memories of the shaky footage of a young president in a convertible, his wife cradling his head in the lap of her pink suit. As the assassination retired Pearl Harbor, 9/11 retired the assassination. History is the fateful push of time.

This trail of memories was rekindled as I listened to the accounts last week on Radio 4 of the bombings of Nagasaki and Hiroshima. The pilot of the *Enola Gay* told how the bomb dropped on Hiroshima was called 'Little Boy', how the aircraft performed a sharp 155-degree turn and dived 518 metres, that the bomb exploded 576 metres above the city. Embedded in the details: the voices of survivors describing the day in their lives when history was pulverised and time stopped.

Although those weapons of mass destruction exploded before I was born, I was aware of these dates from an early age: my birthday is on the anniversary of Nagasaki. There is something embarrassing about sharing a birthday with one of these fateful dates. On 9/11, I was in London for a dinner with my friend Betsy Drake. I called her in the late afternoon, thinking that with such tragic news we should cancel our plans, but she had spent a disciplined day at her desk and knew nothing. 'Please come,' she said after I told her, adding, 'it's my birthday.' Months later she told me that 'the date is unbearable. I'm officially changing my birthday to September 1.'

When Jackie Kennedy first saw the plans for the World Trade Center she lamented: 'they're stealing the sky.' Now

I'd put it like this: tragic dates are stealing our calendar and it's hard to live life in a permanent diary of grief. I tried not to let the phrase '7/7' slide into my vocabulary. It feels like a victory for the dehumanised bombers to give them a day.

It probably helps that the countryside operates on a calendar that doesn't recognise dates. Cows have to be milked twice daily, hay must be made while the sun shines. True, only a tiny sliver of the rural population now makes hay, but the cultural legacy is still agriculture. People are more alarmed at the filth of their hospital wards and nursing staff who do not speak English than they are by the murderous quagmire of the Middle East. They worry more about the price of oil than they do about the plundered planet. Farmers in the Fens feel more threatened by the buying power of Tesco than by al-Qaeda. Which doesn't mean that country life is parochial, only that you have to live life a day at a time. No one has the courage to say 'never again'.

August 18, 2005

LAISSEZ LES BON TEMPS ROULER

WHENEVER I have a case of the blues, I take a ham hock and a pound of spicy smoked sausage out of the freezer and put two cups of red beans in a pan to soak. Thawing and soaking take eight hours, cooking another two, but red beans and rice provide comfort that passeth all understanding.

'Red beans and rice' is part of my culture. It's also the culture of New Orleans, our 'big town', my family's escape hatch, our spiritual watering hole: a 100-mile journey that delivered Mississippians out of their 'dry' state to the amphibious city where liquor flowed and the motto was *'laissez les bon temps rouler'* (let the good times roll). Last October I bought 10lb of red beans from the French Market and a bag of filé, the powdered leaves of the sassafras tree used to flavour my other edible cure, seafood gumbo.

Today, while the red beans soak, I listen to the radio, read the papers and press the redial button. For three days my calls have been met with: 'All telephone lines are down. Please try later.' Last night, news as tangled as the mimosa and bougainvillea in the city's steamy grotto gardens began to emerge via emails: my cousin Jamie, whose flat is on Conti Street in the French Quarter, was safe out in California; cousin Steve's house between Gulfport and Biloxi is damaged but still standing. English friends whose daughter Catherine teaches at Tulane report that she stayed in New Orleans until Tuesday night because she didn't want to leave her two dogs. Finally, friends drove her and the dogs to Baton Rouge, picking up another distressed dog on the way.

Every few hours I go to www.nola.com to read the New Orleans *Times-Picayune*, the city's newspaper, whose presses are all under water. The lead article begins: 'No one can say they didn't see it coming...' That rings true. Last October, sitting in the Café du Monde eating *beignets* and drinking chicory-flavoured coffee, I read a report issued in 2001 by the Federal Emergency Management Agency warning that a hurricane striking New Orleans was one of the three most likely disasters in the US. (The other was a terrorist attack on New York City; I've forgotten the third.) But by 2003, the federal funding for flood control was diverted to the war in Iraq. In 2004, the Bush administration cut by 80% funding requested for holding back the brackish waters of Lake Pontchartrain. Meanwhile, developers were destroying wetlands and barrier islands that surround New Orleans, areas that historically have held back the surge of hurricanes.

But if a storm as Biblical in its fury as Hurricane Katrina was predictable, no one could have predicted the fatal delay in establishing order, organising shelter, food, drinking water, tents, lights, sanitation and the descent into violence and anarchy.

No one now remembers the Great Mississippi Flood of 1927 when a million people lost their homes and black sharecroppers spent months on top of a levee without adequate food, shelter or medical care. My grandfather, a Delta planter, saw the '27 flood as a parable of ineptitude and greed. He believed that natural disasters expose man-made injustices, wash away the foundations of one society and plant the roots of another. The world is now witness to a powerful country's long-hidden darkness to the limits of power. They say that New Orleans will never be the same. I don't know that America will ever be the same.

September 8, 2005

SIMPLE GIFTS

THIS morning I went to a memorial service for Rosa Parks. I didn't have to go far, just down the drive to a cottage built in the 1920s. Although it has moved with the times (indoor bathroom, central heating), the cottage has a simplicity that she would have approved of.

The first thing I did was to make a pot of coffee. I don't think she would have minded that. On the night she was arrested for refusing to surrender her seat to a white passenger, she returned home to the small apartment she shared with her husband and her mother. They were joined by E. D. Nixon, the NAACP leader in Montgomery who'd paid the $100 bail, and two white Alabamans, Virginia and Clifford Durr. Cliff was a lawyer who had worked in Washington during the New Deal, and Virginia was a belle with a deep hatred of southern bigotry. For three hours that night, they drank coffee and discussed what to do next. Finally, Cliff asked Mrs Parks if she wanted to test

133

the constitutionality of the law itself or if she wanted him to try and get her off on the fact that the bus driver hadn't been following the law. Her husband was reluctant: 'Rosa, the white folks will kill you.' But she said she wanted to test the constitutionality of the law. That solemn reply triggered a bus boycott that catapulted Martin Luther King into the national spotlight and changed the history of America forever.

Coffee in hand, I gaze at the book-lined shelves that surround the cottage 'reading room', which looks over wheat fields. I take down the books that I want as my texts for the service. First of all, her own: *Rosa Parks: My Story*. Then Virginia Foster Durr's *Outside the Magic Circle: Autobiography*. And, of course, *Stride Toward Freedom*, Martin Luther King's moving account of what happened in Montgomery, Alabama, after one small, meticulous woman stayed seated.

On top of my pile is a slender volume in the Penguin Lives series by Douglas Brinkley, an eloquent book that makes it clear that the seamstress who earned $23 a week altering men's clothes did not stumble into the civil rights movement by accident, but had spent her whole life building the physical and moral courage to demand her civil rights.

The music for this solitary service is Bryn Terfel's *Simple Gifts*. As I read, I listen to the Welsh baritone singing the words of the spiritual *Deep River*:

O don't you want to go to that gospel feast,
That promised land where all is peace.

Although I call it the library, what's housed here is a modest 'collection' of the histories, biographies and memoirs of a period of American history. All the books and papers will eventually go off to Oxford University, to the Rothermere American Institute. I should part with it soon, but today I find comfort in its presence. It gives me a chance to visit again the Durrs, whom I knew, and to say farewell to Rosa Parks who spent her whole life trying to educate young people. On the evening she was arrested, she was due to run her weekly NAACP Youth Council meeting at the tiny Lutheran church across the street. I think that she would be glad this period of American history is finding a home in England. She found pleasure in quoting Joel 1:3: 'Tell it to your children, and let your children tell it to their children, and their children to the next generation.'

November 3, 2005

EGGNOG AND FRUITCAKE

MY Christmas begins on a cold evening early in December with the first batch of eggnog. After I shut up the chickens, feed the dogs and light the fire, I ladle out the eggnog into a glass that has an inch of bourbon in the bottom. I stir it and grate a crust of nutmeg on top. Then I sit down with my copy of *A Christmas Memory*, a bittersweet story by Truman Capote about a dreamy seven-year-old boy making fruitcakes for Christmas with his beloved sixty-something cousin.

The story takes place in the Thirties, but time used to move slowly in the rural South, and the smell of the kitchen, the feel of the cold air, is as familiar to me as my grandmother's kitchen. As I read and drink, my own Christmas memories kick in. Like Buddy's cousin in the story, my grandmother could kill a rattlesnake with a hoe and tame hummingbirds. And like Buddy and his cousin, every year we went to the bootlegger to get bourbon for her fruitcakes.

Those trips signalled the beginning of Christmas. Old Mr Piggot would come out to the car and lean courteously over the car window. A tall, gaunt man with only one arm – he'd lost the other one in the cotton gin – he didn't make moonshine, he simply 'imported' whiskey from Tennessee in the trunk of his car. My grandmother always told him she'd come for 'whiskey for my fruitcakes', and Mr Piggot softly replied to the widow of the county prosecuting attorney, 'Yes, ma'am, I know that.'

Unlike Buddy's cousin, my grandmother would never have sent a fruitcake to President Roosevelt, but she wouldn't have sent a cake to President Bush, either. Her cakes, like her generosity, were for 'family' only.

Now all that's left of that world is my Great-Aunt Edna, the youngest of the five sisters. She turned 100 in October and lives with Aunt Ruby, who is 70-something. You still can't buy bourbon in Scott County, which remains steadfastly 'dry', and the nearest 'wet' county is 50 miles away.

'Honey, we've got something better than bourbon,' Aunt Edna tells me when I call. 'We bought a generator!' After Hurricane Katrina, they were without electricity for 10 days.

'This is our Christmas present to ourselves. We just went wild!' My great-aunt is the curator of our family, the last one left who remembers all of us as children, the genealogist who's never done research, just remembers.

She's also the only grown-up who never yelled at us, was never impatient or unkind.

When Sam was small, I used to read this story to him, stopping to tell him when Capote's story dovetailed with my own. Now, at 16, he's happy for me to take this sentimental journey on my own. Instead, we'll drive to Cambridge and see *Capote*, a film described in today's paper as 'beautifully austere and morally searching'. It tells how the elfin boy of *A Christmas Memory* came to write and publish *In Cold Blood*. Time moves on.

By the time I've finished my second glass of eggnog, I wish I had the nerve, the energy, the imagination, to create a viable other kind of Christmas for Sam. A Christmas that begins with a spooky trip to the bootlegger, and fruitcakes that never contain anything red or green. A Christmas where he earns money picking pecans (25 cents for each full lard bucket) and spends every Saturday searching for the perfect present. A Christmas preceded by months and months of yearning. A Christmas morally searching and beautifully austere.

December 1, 2005

III
Crop Rotation

THE LIMOUSINE QUARTET

ON the Friday before Christmas, a limousine longer than the Norwich-to-London train pulled into the farm car park. The four men who got out did not look like lottery winners or rock stars. They didn't even look festive, just contented – in a bankerish, lawyerish way. They had booked a table for four in the restaurant, but when I saw the limo I realised it was a special occasion and raced ahead to ask Tony, shop manager and flower artist, to come up with something special fast. The *Viburnum x bodnantense* had been frosted the night before, but it had to do. If we'd only known, we could have done better.

Limousines aren't really a country thing, especially in winter with all the mud from the sugar-beet lorries, potholes and pheasant roadkill. You'd have thought a Cadillac had pulled up at Cold Comfort Farm, as one by one all the shop, kitchen and restaurant staff sneaked out to have a look at the sleek machine, longer than a combine, lower than a plough.

That the limousine roused more interest than the table of four says something about just how sophisticated we are these days here on the prairies of East Anglia. Because the limousine quartet was our first 'civil ceremony' lunch: groom and groom and two witnesses. I'm not one of those patrons who regularly swans around meeting and greeting, but I rise to occasions. When I went over to say hello, I was told that the happy couple had been together for 37 years.

Relationships that endure for nearly four decades touch something in me. I treasure a heart-shaped ruby brooch left to me by my mother-in-law, given to her on her ruby anniversary, first presented to her mother-in-law on her ruby anniversary. I haven't yet reached half a ruby, but I've been here long enough to have a pretty good idea of the commitment, love, tolerance and work required to reach those milestones. I felt relieved that these two people sitting in the restaurant would now be able to visit one another in intensive care, benefit from pensions and insurance policies, and live their lives a little freer of institutional prejudice.

I edited Leviticus out of my belief system long ago, along with 'Intelligent Design', the notion that the universe could only have been designed by an intelligent being. Although I'm the granddaughter and wife of dedicated Darwinists, I'm not a strict and pure Darwinist. I think of myself as a Puffinist. For one thing, puffins marry for life. Although no puffin can tell the difference between other

144

puffins – no telltale laugh, no adorable flutter of wing, no unforgettable feathery face – they have a passionate loyalty to place. Their heart is where their burrow is. For most of the year they have a loner's temperament, floating about in solitary seascape. Then, come spring, Puffinville becomes like *Sex and the City*: brief encounters with no strings attached. Finally, bored and tired, they come down to earth (literally) to the grassy slopes dotted with puffin burrows. Within hours, the puffin couple is reunited in the same burrow they occupied the year before. This fidelity to place, so powerful yet so practical, produces baby puffins and marriages that last till death does them part.

Puffins seem to find this way of life unremarkable and comforting. There is much to be said for the comfort of the burrow. I reckon that, by removing the legal limbo, civil ceremonies will affirm the ordinariness and privilege of commitment; provide the comfort of difficult, ordinary happiness. Long live the Puffinhood.

January 19, 2006

THE PATHOS OF LOST THINGS

THE day after Mr Hare (B.D.S., B.Sc., M.G.D.S., F.D.S.R.C.S. (Eng) – Specialist in Surgical Dentistry) pulled my tooth, the tree surgeons cut down our walnut tree. Tooth and tree were twins in death. The theme of this story is loss.

The tooth fatality began at a candlelit dinner nearly two decades ago, a shooting weekend (when we still had those). I chomped down on a piece of lead shot nestled in the tender breast of an English partridge (when we still had those). I'm not of the Stiff Upper Lip school, but I abide by George Washington's *Rules of Civility and Decent Behaviour*: at table do not 'Scratch, Spit, Cough or blow your Nose except there's a Necessity for it'. I reckon America's first president thought 'do not Swear or Holler' went without saying. What is permissible in the English gentry is the visible retrieval of the piece of lead shot, careful examination, the announcement to fellow diners, 'Ah, a piece of shot', followed by a melodic ping as it is dropped on to the Spode side plate. The more audible the ping, the more substantial the commitment to one's dentist.

Mine is based in the neighbouring village of Hopton. Jo Hassan's practice, part NHS, part private, includes all my family, half my payroll and a real duke. Truly, no one has been more dedicated in the quest to save my cracked tooth. But this was no benign molar, just a born trouble-maker. It began to pull away from its neighbour, creating a hiding place for those pesky morsels that squeeze in like hedgehogs in a chicken house. My tongue, after years of dislodging the meaty little perpetrators, could now pull a plough.

Still, I thought that my tooth and I had made a truce: I'd mind the gap and the tooth would remain pain-free. But Mrs Hassan warned me there is no *détente* in the dental wars. A troubled tooth is like global warming: calamitous if not dealt with. The tooth had to go.

When you call your farm diversification 'The Leaping Hare', there is something reassuring about a dental surgeon called Mr Hare. I also value propinquity: his practice is on Guildhall Street in Bury St Edmunds. On the morning of my appointment, I stocked up on Anadin Extra (my mother's motto was: 'There is no dignity in pain') and eight pots of Duchy Originals Beetroot Soup (delicious). Mr Hare talks you through it: 'Dentists don't actually "pull" teeth out. They rock the tooth slowly side to side until the bone surrounding it expands and the ligament breaks, allowing it to slide out.' I didn't want to hurt his feelings by interrupting him but, in this instance, ignorance is bliss.

In fact, once he began to 'not' pull , the whole procedure took less than five minutes.

What lasts rather longer is the sense of loss. As the tree surgeons carefully extracted the decayed roots of the walnut tree, I guiltily studied my options: a 'tooth-coloured bridge' (from £335) or an implant (£2,163), a tree resistant to honey fungus.

All week long, I've been gazing at the gaping hole where the once proud tree stood, anxiously avoiding the gaping hole where my trusty, hunky molar lived. I confessed to my friend Katie that I have begun to dream of George Washington and his wooden dentures.

'Eejit,' she says, 'that's just urban legend. Washington had two sets of false teeth, both carved from the finest hippopotamus ivory and gold. The set loaned to the Smithsonian in 1976 for the bicentennial was stolen and never recovered.'

When your theme is loss, your cup runneth over.

January 26, 2006

BOOKS REVISITED

THE card that I send to friends with new babies is a drawing by Paris Bottman of a maternal hare holding a pair of baby socks. The message reads: 'Lucky you! Now you have a reason to buy those wonderful little booties... and little undershirts, and little gowns, and little hats.' There is something hard-wired in the female brain that loves buying little undershirts, little wellies and little sweaters, and it's a sad moment when little is over. I'm hanging on to the little wellie museum that lines the front porch, a tender souvenir of *temps perdus* that has survived every clear-your-clutter campaign. The little feet that once fitted into the frog wellies, the 'ellie' wellies and the cowboy boots are now a size 12 and prefer shoes from Shipton & Heneage.

So I have to meet my maternal urges in other ways. A sequel to the card could read: 'Lucky you! Now you have a reason to re-read all those books you loved as you embark on AS Level English by proxy.' All week long I've been re-reading *A Passage to India* in sync with

149

Sam's required reading and Samuel West's reading of it on *Book at Bedtime*. This total immersion has been far more compelling than my first go 35 years ago. I am astonished by how much I missed. Was I so ignorant? Was I reading against the deadline of the essay? I remember the plot, but I missed the subtlety, the poetry, the radical conclusions.

The winter term AS reading list took me on a return journey to *Brideshead Revisited*. Perhaps I'm less in awe of the aristocratic glamour than I was when I first read it, and I find all the Catholic bits – the Big Theme – rather tedious and suspect (I'm blessed with Catholic friends who are not tormented by their faith), but I no longer believe in the story. Waugh wrote it during the war while recovering from a parachuting accident, and I first read the 1945 edition. My re-reading is the 1959 edition that Waugh cut substantially and to which he made a few additions. In the preface, he confesses to infusing the book with a 'kind of gluttony, for food and wine, for the splendours of the past, and for rhetorical and ornamental language, which now, with a full stomach, I find distasteful.' Still, the alcoholism, the snobbery, the adultery, and the yearning for a vanished world, give the book an unexpected timelessness.

There is something spooky about re-reading books you have loved. I reckon it is a little like friendsreunited.com: it might be exciting to get back in touch with the once-handsome football player, but it might also be excruciating. I know that Jane Austen never disappoints, but Colette does. Re-reading Angus Wilson works for me; re-reading Martin Amis does not. Trollope: yes, Thackeray: no. So much depends on who you were during the first rapturous reading. We swoon less with time.

Every few years I re-read F. Scott Fitzgerald's *The Crack-Up*, the writer's melancholy account of his nervous breakdown. He begins with a general observation – 'the test of a first-rate intelligence is the ability to hold two opposed ideas in the mind at the same time, and still retain the ability to function. One should, for example, be able to see that things are hopeless and yet be determined to make them otherwise.' That description is my spiritual sudoku, my daily IQ test. For example: this Government is content to see the countryside vanish, to be transformed into housing estates and storage warehouses, and yet I spend my days trying to keep a farm and a landscape intact. In order not to crack up, I spend my evenings re-reading the books of my vanished youth.

February 2, 2006

SWAN SONG

ONE morning in December, as I lay in bed doing inventory of the day ahead, Sam rushed into the room: 'Get up! You have to get up now!' He'd spotted something on Lake Bofus, the smaller of our two lakes, that I had to see. There wasn't time to dress, so I put my old overcoat over my nightdress, stepped into cold wellies and followed Sam across the icy fields. Silently, we scrambled up the steep bank that shelters the lake on one side, Sam leading the way to an opening through the Norfolk reeds. There in front of us was a scene of such beauty and tranquility that we stood in a frozen hush of awe and wonder – a swan and her two babies. Gangly adolescents, really, the colour of *lattes*. We stared at them. They stared at us. Unperturbed, they seemed content to monitor our presence as they continued their parade of graceful, deliberate insouciance.

All week long, we went back to visit, sometimes four times a day. It confused the dogs, this ritual of going off without them, but we didn't want anything to disturb the swans, to make them, in their innocence and serenity, feel unwelcome. We felt honoured by these beautiful wild birds that had chosen our lake. One evening, I looked up the poem by W. B. Yeats that I once knew by heart but now couldn't remember – *The Wild Swans at Coole*:

> But now they drift on the still water
> Mysterious, beautiful;
> Among what rushes will they build,
> By what lake's edge or pool
> Delight men's eyes, when I awake some day
> To find they have flown away?

And then, one morning, they were gone. We were sad but not as broken-hearted as we would have been if we had found bloodstained grass and white feathers, the signature of the fox that took all my Call ducks. We were grateful for this interlude with these great wild birds, and we hoped they would remember our watery haven and honour us with a return journey.

We continued to brood on the swans, especially on the ancient belief that the souls of poets pass into swans at their deaths. Virgil was known as the 'Mantuan Swan', and Homer was 'The Swan of Meander'. Ben Jonson called Shakespeare 'The Swan of Avon'. I don't know if Yeats had a swan attached to his name, but in Ireland they revere swans, and believe that if a man kills a swan he will die within the year.

The memory of the Christmas swans came back to me this week, with the news of the deaths of swans from the H5N1 strain of avian flu. This morning, the disease was confirmed in dead swans in Italy and Austria. Epidemiologists speculate that the nesting places of the migrating swans – the rivers and lakes – have become dumping grounds for chicken manure. Even when the manure, mountains of it from intensive poultry farming, isn't dumped on the land, it leeches into the ground water.

Conventional wisdom tells us that avian flu, like Hurricane Katrina, isn't our fault. That Nature is capricious and cruel. I admit that Nature is complicated: you have swans, and you have foxes and rats; you have the Sahara and you have Antarctica. But I can't help the melancholy feeling that we, not the swans, have made a mess of the planet. The world is short on poets. Now we may be short on those majestic birds that some cultures believe embody the human soul. When the swans return, we will watch them with trembling hearts.

February 23, 2006

A LEGACY OF TRUTH AND JUSTICE

A COLD, grey morning that begins in the kitchen, the only warm room in the house. I grind the coffee beans, pour milk into a jug, let the coffee steep. Every move is a silent homage to my friend Sybille, who was serious about anything involving ritual and skills. Finally, I open the papers to the obituaries. *Times*, *Telegraph* and *Guardian*. A full page in each, large photographs with Sybille's unflinching gaze. Except for the profile shot in *The Telegraph* with the caption 'Sybille Bedford reading in the marble bath of her penthouse in Rome in 1950, photographed by her lover Evelyn Glendel'. What pictures don't show: eyes as blue as the Mediterranean; pale, wispy hair as soft as the bottom feathers of chickens.

Obituaries set the record straight: born in Charlottenburg, outside Berlin, in 1911, only daughter of a feckless half-English mother and a German aristocratic father. We were friends for a quarter of a century before I knew Sybille's maiden name was von Schoenebeck. I knew that Aldous and Maria Huxley had arranged a marriage for her in the Thirties so that she could become a British citizen. But if she was reticent on the subject of Walter Bedford, she was grateful for his plain English name.

In the mid-Eighties Sybille and I made a journey to Berlin, her first for 50 years. In the no-man's land of Checkpoint Charlie, she became mute with fear, slowly reviving over lunch with relatives who lived in the East, but only recovering when we were back in West Berlin at the Cafe de Paris, a French restaurant that served impeccable *entrecôte grillé*, *pommes frites* and Fleurie served *frais*. She refused to eat anywhere else.

Sybille's decision to write in English – her third language after German and French – gave her words the rich unexpectedness found in Isak Dinesen and Joseph Conrad. She conquered her adopted language, becoming a Fellow of the Royal Society of Literature, receiving an OBE. In 1992, she was made a Companion of Literature, this country's highest honour – there are only ever 10 at any time.

Sybille came to my wedding, but predicted that marriage and country life 'will take up a lot of time'. Our quarterly dinners dwindled to annual dinners, although whenever I was in London I dropped off rabbit terrines, *confits* of duck and partridge, slabs of Suffolk ham. Her heart sank when people sent flowers – she begrudged anything that was not edible or *buvable* coming into her tiny flat on Old

156

Church Street. On her 90th birthday, I gave her a modest 'lifetime' monthly wine allowance at Lea and Sandeman. In return, she gave me grateful and detailed wine reports, laced with gossip.

In June last year, when her memoir was published, she complained that the reviews praising her book read 'like obituaries'. The reviews left out the most important relationship in Sybille's life: her translator and close companion, Aliette Martin. For years, this French woman converted Sybille's hieroglyphics (she was, by then, too frail to type) on to disks. Without Aliette's devotion, intelligence and care, *Quicksands* would still be an indecipherable sheaf of pale green papers.

Sybille regretted that her books were praised and honoured but never profitable. Plagued by 'doubt, despair and sloth', she also regretted the meagreness of her output (12 volumes all the same), that too many years passed 'in idleness, in pleasures, in much private grief'. They say that when a person dies they take a whole world with them. For her friends and readers, Sybille leaves a world behind. Call it a legacy.

March 2, 2006

GARDENER, WRITER, FRIEND

THE invitation sits on my desk, the indigo blue shirt and bright red hand-knit waistcoat as vibrant as his Long Border in June. And the face in full sun, a halo of white hair and a smile that has just stifled a chuckle. The message reads: 'Christo wanted his friends to celebrate his life. He would have wanted you to be there, so bring your fond memories of him, and come and join the party.'

Christopher Lloyd forbade any memorial service, but he wanted a party on what would have been his 85th birthday. And so, on Saturday, I took the train to Great Dixter. A cold, sunny day in early March, the first sight on entering the front gate was planned by Christo: a carpet of Dutch crocuses.

The horticulturally grand, the great and the good of the gardening world were there: Beth Chatto, Anna Pavord, Roy Lancaster, Joy Larkcom, Sarah Raven, as well as the not-yet-famous young people whom Christo encouraged, educated and enjoyed. A generous host who cooked and

158

served memorable meals, Christo loved filling Great Dixter with friends. On Saturday, it felt like he was there: vivid photographs by Jonathan Buckley of Christo and his beloved dachshund, Canna; Christo and Fergus Garrett, 'my head gardener and closest friend'; Christo, Fergus and Anne Wright, his devoted sub-editor at COUNTRY LIFE, looked out on his friends gathered in the Great Hall. Christo's parents used this magnificent timber-framed hall as their dining and living room until the Second World War. Christo used it for large dinner parties, although it is a fair trek to the kitchen and he was the cook.

One of a passing breed, Christo lived the whole of his long life in the house where he was born. In many ways, Great Dixter looks like time has stood still since Lutyens designed the additions to the house and laid out the garden in 1911. But Christo believed that gardeners should 'live on the frontier of their experience', and was always keen to discover something new and exciting, finding space at Dixter for the works of contemporary potters, writers and furniture makers. He felt privileged to live at Great Dixter, writing: 'I tried to deserve my luck by taking my responsibilities seriously. Dixter is a lovely place to live in and for others it is an oasis.'

After a lunch that would have pleased Christo, a stroll around the famous garden. Around each corner, I expected to see his colourful shape, weeding or checking out the survival skills of a tender plant. At tea-time, we gathered in the Great Hall to listen to Christo's recording in August 2000 of *Desert Island Discs*. What pleasure to hear his beautiful deep voice, his outspoken sense of humour and his choice of music. Christo's love of music was only surpassed by his love of plants. He began with Poulenc's oboe sonata, before weaving his life through Bach, Mozart, Brahms and Janácek. And when forced to choose: Bach's *Goldberg Variations*; *The Letters of Gustave Flaubert*; a ceaseless supply of his beloved 'Syndicate' Scotch whisky.

A few years ago Christo was diagnosed with Parkinson's disease. It was a mistaken diagnosis, and a triple bypass operation gave him renewed energy and optimism. He set about creating the Great Dixter Charitable Trust so that the garden could continue to inspire and educate. Knowing that Dixter was in the capable hands of Fergus gave him happy peace of mind. Knowing that Great Dixter lives on also goes a long way in filling the hole left in the lives of Christo's readers and friends.

March 16, 2006

THOUGHTS OF A MELANCHOLY OPTIMIST

FOUR days after my grandfather's funeral, my grandmother made a bonfire of all the books in his library she considered 'subversive'. These included the complete works of Darwin, a stack of books by the agnostic humanist Robert Ingersoll, and an entire shelf of novels by a Southern writer called James Branch Cabell. My grandfather saw in Cabell's mythical medieval world a satire on the contradictions of life in the South. My grandmother believed the books were pornographic. I wouldn't know. I was barely tackling *Huck Finn* when Cabell and Co were burned at the stake. Or, more accurately, in the smokehouse. I reckon my taste for the subversive came from eating hams smoked with the thoughts of Darwin, Thomas Paine, William Cobbett and Cabell.

I still haven't read Cabell. Medieval Romanticism is not my thing. Still, imagine my surprise at seeing a poster this week in Liverpool Street station with the message: 'The optimist proclaims that we live in the best of all possible worlds; and the pessimist fears this is true' – James Branch Cabell, from *The Silver Stallion*, 1926. The quote latched on to me like a tick.

If I start the day watching the Jacob and Shetland lambs jiving in the front meadow, I say a grateful prayer for this best of all possible worlds. But when I wake up to *Farming Today* and the desperate voices of England's farmers sinking into a quagmire of debt due to the disastrous mishandling of the Rural Payments Agency, pessimism closes in like fog.

When I let the chickens out of their enclosure, once a Palais de Poulets, now a Guantanamo Bay, I buck and snort about Defra which has refused us the vaccine that every major country in the EU has accepted. In an impersonation of optimism I remind myself that a human pandemic caused by H5N1 is by no means inevitable, that the virus does not infect people easily. That tens of millions of birds have been infected, but fewer than 200 people. Optimism holds until a late-morning scan of an article from the *New York Times* forwarded by a fellow henkeeper. Entitled 'How Serious is the Risk?', it ends with advice from the Center for Disease Control in Atlanta: to be safe, hold off on buying imported feather pillows, down coats and duvets. I remember words from Ingersoll rolled out by my farming grandfather during hot, rainless summers: 'In nature, there are neither rewards nor punishments. There are consequences.'

'Forget bird flu,' a cousin emails me. 'If you're wanting pessimism, think Iran.' 'Look, the planet is 4,500,000,000 years old,' he writes. 'Nuclear weapons have been around for 61. Until now, they haven't been in the hands of suicidal fanatics fueled by religious ideology.' He's adamant: Iran is the most dangerous problem facing the planet.

'What about global warming? Isn't that the apocalypse now?' I type back.

'The world is waking up to the anger of global warming. Even Evangelical Christians and Walmart are waking up. But the world is still dopey about President Ahmadinejad who's developing nuclear weapons and says the end of history is only two or three years away. He claims that the appearance of the 12th Iman, Shi'ism's version of the Messiah, is imminent.'

As I spray the belly buttons of the newborn lambs, I compose a letter to Radio 4: 'Dear Sirs, Perhaps it's time to replace "Thought for the Day" with "Fear for the Day". You might consider Mr Cabell for *Book at Bedtime*.'

Yours truly,

Hope against Hope.

April 6, 2006

THE LAST ICEBERG

A CLOSE friend says that being in Alcoholics Anonymous is like observing Lent all year round: denial, meditation, confession, repentance. She tells me this because each year I contemplate giving up wine for Lent. I never do. She, who has given up wine for life, believes that denial needs a framework. 'Like Lenten complines, an evening a week with others. Otherwise sacrifice gets lost in private dailyness.'

This year, I embarked on an equally difficult programme of denial, a vow not to buy anything unnecessary. Not the flowery linen skirt that spoke to me of spring, nor the divine taupe shoes. Not even the tempting catalogue to the *Americans in Paris* exhibition.

As Lent was originally only three days, I gave myself a mid-way reprieve during our few days in Scotland. The trip was the pay-off to a promise we'd made to Sam: do well in your GCSEs, and two days' fishing on the Tay will be yours. And my reward: a pilgrimage to The

Watermill in Aberfeldy, the bookshop/gallery/music-and-coffee shop that is my personal Compostela. I negotiated my timeslot at The Watermill as carefully as Sam organised his ghillie, and I arrived at the same pitch of excitement that he feels on a salmon river.

But before I reached the shelves, I saw a notice for the exhibition in the gallery on the top floor of the bookshop. 'Ice and Light: Antarctica'. My heart stopped.

My fascination for Antarctica began on Putney Heath. For four years, I lived in a first-floor flat at No. 7, Heathview Gardens. Although no blue plaque identified the house, this was the London home of Ernest Shackleton, and the week I moved in (December 1981) a snow storm transformed the Heath into a polar wonderland. My neighbour, a mountaineering lawyer named John Harding, loaned me his copy of *South*, Shackleton's account of his crew's struggle for survival after their ship was crushed, leaving them stranded on ice floes in the Weddell Sea. Although I knew the harrowing stories of Scott's expedition, I'd barely heard of Shackleton. After reading *South*, I tracked down everything I could find about Scott, Oates, Shackleton – and Frank Hurley, whose photographs and diary of Shackleton's 1914 voyage to Antarctica are the most beautiful and haunting images in my mind's visual museum.

Until, that is, I stood in the small gallery in Aberfeldy and looked at the paintings by Malize McBride. The artist's fascination with Antarctica began with her father's copy of Apsley Cherry-Garrard's book *The Worst Journey in the World*, the sad account by the youngest member on Scott's journey to the South Pole. That book was the beginning of her longing to see Antarctica, a desire weighed down by guilt: the pressure on that fragile environment from tourism is huge. Only when McBride was reassured by the severe limits on access did she go there herself in January 2004.

I arrived on the last day of the exhibition. A few pictures were unsold, including the largest, some 8ft wide, called *Last Iceberg*. Majestic, silent, contemplative, it spoke of those explorers: brave, optimistic, bookish men, eating stewed penguin and reading Tennyson. And, inevitably, of how the well-being of our planet depends on these skyscrapers of ice. In a few days, *Last Iceberg* will hang in my house. Not in keeping with vows, but a Lenten meditation on what the men who encountered these ice mountains knew: fortune gives us nothing that we can really own.

April 13, 2006

IN LOVING MEMORY

WE decided that Easter Monday would be a good day to consecrate the graveyard. The house was still full of ecumenical friends who wouldn't have soul issues, but could bring sufficient solemnity to the occasion. By 'consecrate', I mean declaring something sacred, not dedicating to a religious purpose. All the same, garden visitors wandering through the gate might be confused by so many wooden crosses dotting this shady, enclosed space. It looks like a recent rural tragedy.

In fact, the crosses are a sad testament to the haphazard nature of our animal husbandry. The most recent cross marks the grave of Derrick, our Norfolk Black turkey, blessed with curiosity, humour and playfulness. His last game was a session of ice hockey on the garden pond, but the mild winter meant the frozen surface could not support his 34lb heft. He is buried next to my quartet of Call ducks, which met a more commonplace doom: killed by the fox. Beneath the fresh mound is a lamb rejected by her mama. Another cross presides over the remains of my most majestic peacock, Emanuel, who died in the middle of the total solar eclipse in August 1999.

Against the backdrop of handmade crosses and walls of yew hedge punctuated with columns of Irish yew are three new oak headstones with handcarved lettering. Like the graveyards of my youth, these more significant – although pure and simple – ones mark the greater status: long-lived and long-loved dogs and cats. The first one reads: 'Adam, noble dog, 1982–1996'. Adam, my dowry and my husband's first dog. After a happy childhood on Putney Heath, he became a country dog, learned to retrieve pheasants, and became the loving companion of the cat who rests beside him.

'Pushkin, self-made cat'. Pushkin, who lived wild in the potato harvester before making her way up to the Big House, showing feline canniness by making friends with the Only Child, then aged two. Within six months, she was napping alongside Adam in front of the AGA and sleeping on the foot of our bed. I've never subscribed to the phoney belief that folks are either cat people or dog people: I love both.

Still, I suspect that Adam was sometimes homesick for Putney Heath. He had more friends there, including a black lab called Tatler, whose owner, the distinguished soldier, Lt-Gen Sir Henry Leask, gave valuable advice to a devoted band of female dog walkers. The General's deepest wish was for a heaven where he would be reunited with the horses and dogs of his life, a sentiment shared by the Texan Joe Murray, who wrote: 'Wouldn't it be wonderful to arrive in heaven and find that the angels are dogs, that the dogs we had in our life on Earth had been our guardian angels.'

I'm definitely of the Murray-Leask school on this, but go one further: I want to be buried beside my dogs. The Wyken graveyard is no 'pet cemetery', but a family graveyard. I'm okay about boxes of ashes, wicker coffins – whatever is environmentally correct at the time – but, as I have been too scattered all my life, I have no desire for my ashes to be scattered over fields or sea.

The Wyken graveyard makes my husband a little nervous. He tells Simon the gardener that 'it's a Southern thing'. I decide to wait a while before I show him my design for the lychgate. Simply carved on its Gothic arch: 'A Living Dog is Better than a Dead Lion' *Ecclesiates* 9:4.

April 20, 2006

HOMELAND

GOING to see a play that you loved nearly 30 years ago is like having lunch with an old boyfriend. The temptation is irresistible, the chances of disappointment are great. For years Alan Bennett's *The Old Country* has been one of my favourite plays. My memory of Alec Guinness as the English spy living with his wife in exile in the Soviet Union is so clear that I could replay it in my mind. When I learned of the play's revival with Timothy West, I booked tickets immediately.

I'm pretty sure that I missed many of the references back in 1977 when I first saw the play. The utter Englishness of Hilary listening to Elgar probably clicked, but not comparisons of the dacha in the Russian countryside to the stern and wild landscape of John Buchan's Scotland. Hilary's Garrick Club tie would have been lost on me, but not the irony in his take-off of the *Times* obituary column – 'Sir, Might I be permitted to pen a footnote to your (otherwise admirably comprehensive) obituary of Sir Derek (Jack) Clements...'

Other passages feel nicely pertinent now. When Hilary shoots a hare with a revolver from his front porch, his sister calls it a large rabbit. Hilary firmly corrects her: 'They're quite far apart in the evolutionary chain. Further apart than a dog and a fox, for instance. Rabbits are gregarious, slow-moving, leading a rich underground life. Hares are swift, solitary creatures of the open field.' And a wistful lament from Hilary's newly knighted brother-in-law Duff: 'That is something I never do, if I want to sleep at night. Look at back copies of COUNTRY LIFE. The properties. Palaces, practically. Sold for nothing. Ten, even five, years ago. Had one but known...'

The same year I first saw *The Old Country*, a newspaper sent me to interview a real couple in exile. Oswald and Diana Mosley were living near Paris in a miniature château called Le Temple de la Gloire. She had just published her memoir *A Life of Contrasts*. Like Bennett's Hilary and Bron, the Mosleys had a sad air of co-dependence, and Le Temple, despite its Louis XVI furniture, felt like an English country house: *The Times*, *The Spectator* and *The Listener* in the library; Georgian silver on the tea tray; a garden with delphiniums, erect and radiant, rising out of the deep herbaceous borders.

In *The Old Country*, his brother-in-law tries to persuade Hilary to return to England. A short spell in prison, a suitable show of remorse and all would be forgiven. What he would earn from the Sundays would buy a nice cottage in Gloucestershire. Hilary could then write his memoirs. Do *Parkinson*, do *Desert Island Discs*.

The Mosleys served their time in prison before their exile, three-and-a-half years during the war. When they were refused passports in the early Fifties, they escaped to France via Ireland. They never returned to England to live (and never expressed remorse), but occasionally came back. Oswald Mosley actually went to see *The Old Country* on one of his visits to London in the Seventies. He never made it on to *Desert Island Discs*, but Diana did in 1989.

I wonder what an audience will make of *The Old Country* if it is revived in another 30 years' time. The theatre programme will explain Lyon's tea shops and the strange and terrible world of political extremism in the Thirties. The themes of loyalty and betrayal, homeland and exile, friendship and family, may be as timeless as laments for the lost properties of COUNTRY LIFE, but Englishness and its close companions, irony and tolerance, may be lost in the fog of time.

May 4, 2006

172

THE MOCKINGBIRD LEGACY

EVERY so often I wish I had named my son Atticus. He says he's relieved that I didn't, but I reckon he'd have grown to like the name after a while. I had another bout of name-regret this week as I celebrated the 80th birthday of the woman whose Atticus Finch formed my attachment to the name. It was a small party – just me, sitting in the sun, drinking iced tea, eating pound cake and reading out loud to the dogs. It was hard to put together much of a guest list because I can't believe that there's anyone who feels about *To Kill a Mockingbird* the way I do. The fact that the book has been translated into 40 languages and sold 30 million copies worldwide doesn't sway me one bit.

So Harper Lee is 80 years old. In Monroeville, Alabama, where she was born, her friends call her Nelle. She still lives there with her sister, Alice, who is 94 and practises law in the same firm their father joined after he passed the bar exam in 1915. Harper Lee studied law herself but left six months before her final exams to go to New York and become a writer. She even spent a year in England at Oxford, but whatever she thought of the English she's kept to herself. In fact, since she published her one and only book in 1960, she's kept just about everything to herself.

To Kill a Mockingbird is set in Maycomb, Alabama, in the thirties. I grew up in a small southern town called McComb, Mississippi. Between the Thirties and the Fifties not much had changed in these small southern towns that depended mainly on farming and timber. Harper Lee was the same age as her narrator, six-year-old Scout Finch, when the first of the Scottsboro trials began. The crime – the alleged gang rape of two white girls by nine black teenagers on the Southern Railroad freight run from Chattanooga to Memphis on March 25, 1931 – never occurred, but in the Deep South of the Thirties jurors were not willing to accord a black charged with raping a white woman the presumption of innocence. The Scottsboro trials and re-trials would have dominated Harper Lee's childhood, the innocence or guilt of the Scottsboro boys the main subject talked about by the grown-ups, especially in an educated family like the Lees. And it would have fiercely divided the town of Monroeville.

I'm pretty sure of this because when I was Scout's age and Harper Lee's I spent my summers on my grandparents' farm in a little hamlet called Philipp, Mississippi, on the banks of the Tallahatchie River. The day before, I was due to go home to start school, the body of a 14-year-old black boy was found in the river two miles downstream. His name was Emmett Till. His crime was to whistle at a white woman and say 'Bye baby' as he left the country store she and her husband owned, but the trial of the two white men who killed him dominated my childhood. In Mississippi, on a hot September day in 1955, it took the all-white jury just over an hour to return a 'not guilty' verdict.

Like Harper Lee, I came to England for a year. Unlike her, I stayed. I miss the wild, unmanaged childhoods that country children had in the Thirties, the Fifties. I miss the slender grey mockingbirds that know 200 songs, sing their hearts out at a full moon, swoop down and chase cats and dogs for fun, and mate for life. And I miss the sharp sense of justice instilled in us by growing up in families that stuck out because of their belief that, at least in a courtroom, all men are created equal.

May 11, 2006

THE HEART OF THE MATTER

A LITTLE fear resides permanently in the back of my mind: that in an emergency I will dial '911'. Which might alert the emergency services in Hudson, Ohio, but won't be much use here in Suffolk. A card saying '999' taped above the kitchen telephone reminds me where I am, along with memories of the television *999*, with its re-enactments of life or death emergencies. It was the warning voice of Michael Buerk that pushed me to take a course in first aid.

On the first day, the instructor asked how many people died in the Hillsborough Stadium disaster. We gazed silently at the rubber woman on the floor. 'Ninety-six,' came his solemn reply. 'And if people there had known the basic "head-tilt, chin-lift" technique, 70 would have survived.' I don't know if he was right, but the head-tilt, chin-lift is tattooed on my brain: lift the tongue away from the back of the throat and open the airway. Place the patient on his back, then put one hand on the forehead and the fingers of the other hand on the point of the chin. Push down on the forehead and lift up and forward on the chin.

For years, I've been ready to save lives with my head-tilt, chin-lift, although the Heimlich and mouth-to-mouth have faded with time. After I read Joan Didion's account of her husband's heart attack in *The Year of Magical Thinking*, I vowed to take a refresher course, even though his was an instant, massive heart attack that even defibrillating paddles wouldn't have helped. Then, one Saturday morning a few weeks ago, my husband quietly mentioned that he'd been awake at 3am with a chest ache ('Not a pain, an ache'). He then got up early and went for a six-mile bike ride to collect the Saturday papers. The ache returned.

In fact, I didn't call '911' or even '999'. I called our GP's surgery and got one of those weekend call centres. Within 10 minutes, an ambulance was in the drive, the reluctant patient apologising for taking up their time as they attached the ECG tabs to his chest. Minutes later, they were off to the West Suffolk Hospital where the Coronary Care Unit was waiting for him.

As heart attacks go, it was mild. And lucky: the angiogram showed that his main arteries were seriously clogged. Three weeks later, he was at Papworth, where Prof Wallwork performed a coronary-artery-bypass-graft operation, sometimes called a CABG or 'a cabbage', a four-hour procedure where short segments are harvested from a leg vein and attached to the aorta and to points beyond the obstructed areas in each of the narrowed coronary arteries.

'It's like rerouting traffic around a motorway pile-up,' explained the Professor.

That was six days ago. Today, I'm bringing him home. A few weeks ago, the only people I'd heard of who'd had quadruple bypasses were Henry Kissinger, Dick Cheney and Bill Clinton. Now everyone I meet knows someone who has had a 'cabbage', and the Born Again stories sound like Biblical miracles. A staggering 28,000 are performed in the UK each year.

A more troubling statistic: 270,000 people have heart attacks in the UK each year. A third of these die before reaching hospital. When I'm not Googling 'heart disease/coronary bypass', I re-play the scene: me insisting, 'Call the surgery!'; the English-stiff-upper-lip husband arguing, 'I'll wait and see'.

I uncovered a letter written in 1628 by William Harvey M. D. to Charles I: 'The heart of creatures is the foundation of life, the Prince of all, the Sun of their microcosm... from when all vigor and strength does flow.' I've taped it in the kitchen next to '999'.

June 22, 2006

THE BEST OF ROBERT CARRIER

SUMMERTIME, birdsong and sunshine, and then the telephone. Jorn calls to tell me that Robert died in the early hours of the morning.

When someone dies aged 82 it shouldn't come as a surprise, but it does. Especially when he is one of those larger-than-life people who's packed more lives, careers, rooms and countries into his years than most people dream of. But Robert Carrier wasn't 'most' people. An American who came to Europe during the Second World War – he survived the Battle of the Bulge – Robert never shook off the Emersonian notion that the high prize of life is to be born with a bias to some pursuit that finds you in employment and happiness. After the war, he stayed in Europe, mainly France. Then, in 1953, he came to England. Over the next 30 years he changed the way the English cooked and ate. When *The Great Dishes of the World* appeared in 1963, garlic was sold by only one company in London. The book became the manifesto for a revolution that went deeper and lasted longer than the post-war dreams of radical politicians.

By the time I came to live in Suffolk, Robert had sold his restaurant at Hintlesham Hall which he saw in COUNTRY LIFE and bought for £32,000, spending 10 times that to convert it into the luxurious hotel and restaurant that triggered the movement of the country-house hotel. But, like many creative people, Robert found administration rather dull. In the early Eighties, he suddenly decided to sell up and move to Marrakech. His way of writing love letters to a place was to create a sumptuous cookbook, and his *Taste of Morocco* (and, later, *Feasts of Provence*) were just that: passionate, poetic, beautiful books that find the spirit of a place through its culinary soul.

But Robert was too restless for the expatriate life in Morocco. In 1994, aged 70, he returned to England and rented our cottage that overlooks the vineyard. He transformed the kitchen, installed a Lacanche stove, and filmed five television series and wrote six new books. Cream, butter, brandy and truffles were replaced by olive oil, lime juice, ginger as he simplified, lightened and embraced the 21st century.

On his 75th birthday, he told his friends that he missed the south of France. A year later, he moved to L'Isle-sur-la-Sorgue in Provence. When Jorn and I visited him last spring, Robert looked more like 60 than 80 as he showed us his studio. He'd begun painting, and he brought to his new calling his usual iron discipline. Mornings he painted, afternoons and evenings he read in his garden room. Like Goethe's Faust ('Two souls dwell, alas, within my breast') Robert was a contradiction: a culinary populist who was a closet intellectual; a perfectionist who thrived on chaos; a gregarious performer who craved solitude.

Robert taught me how to interview a chef and how to make Mrs Moxon's lemon posset. And he taught me something else. Youth is prolonged by the exaltation of creative effort, but when evening comes take time to enjoy the surrender to peacefulness. For Robert, that meant living within walking distance of a good *charcuterie*, *boulangerie* and wine shop. It meant reading Marcus Aurelius, Montaigne and Seneca, as well as Donna Leon's Venetian thrillers, while listening to Yo-Yo Ma's Bach cello suites. It meant gently filling the hour, and leaving no crevice for repentance or approval. *Merci*, dearest Robert. *Au revoir.*

July 6, 2006

RESERVOIR DREAMS

THE summer evenings are so light and warm that the chickens stay out long past their bedtime. It's nearly nine o'clock before they finally mosey into their *palais des poulets*, an abandoned fruit cage where sheds covered in old car number plates and graffiti by William Blake provide shelter from farmyard terrorists: hedgehogs, foxes and stoats.

The ritual of shutting up chickens makes me feel like a genuine countrywoman. That isn't entirely true. I hate to shoot birds, I am vague on the gestation periods of sheep and cows (eggs hatch out in 28 days, but 28 days from when they are laid or from when the broody broods?), I don't understand why during a long drought the water sucked up by evaporation doesn't return in a cascade of rain, and I owe my knowledge of birdsong to Radio 4. Still, I love the peace of these evenings, the Bach-like chatter of the guinea fowl in their sleeping porches in the apple trees. And every evening this week, following the path of the full moon, I walk over to a field called Cages. I scramble up the small ledge and gaze out on to a field that is being transformed in front of my eyes: dramatic, vast, an earthly miracle.

Ten days ago, Cages was a 10-acre field of oilseed rape which, if we were lucky, would fetch £2,000 when harvested (before seed and labour costs). At the beginning of the week, with the rape crop sacrificed, the topsoil removed and the earth scraped and flattened, the field looked like a magnificent dance floor. It also looked spookily like Prescottville: just pour concrete, build 72 houses and install yellow sodium street lights. With planning permission, this field might be worth more than £20 million. As farmland, it's in a category our bank manager describes as producing 'a level of income insufficient to break even'. In eight weeks' time, it will be a reservoir covering some six acres and holding 20 million gallons of water.

It will also be a debt that will take us 10 years to pay off. Instead of farming concrete – the most profitable crop in the countryside – we have borrowed £98,000 from the bank, the amount we need to match a generous Defra grant (thank you, blessed among taxpayers). The reservoir will enable us to irrigate 150 acres of vegetables. We hope the income from these vegetables will be worth the investment of £1,000 an acre (plus borrowing costs and the nerve-wracking handover of deeds to the bank for 'safekeeping' until the loan is paid).

Under the full moon, I stand in the centre of the amphitheatre and sing at the top of my lungs a song from

Carole King's *Tapestry*: 'I feel the earth move under my feet, I feel the sky tumbling down...' The year 1971 must have been a slow one for me because I know this whole album by heart. The vast cavern of Cages provides its own amplifier, and I move about as nimbly as any ageing rock star, happy to release the nervous energy that accompanies borrowing money and investing in farming.

'If water is the new oil, you've made the right decision,' the farm accountant tells us. I'm not so sure. Reservoirs, like oil fields, can dry up. If we continue turning this corner of East Anglia into a concrete landscape, Cages field will look like a cameo of the Grand Canyon. A reservoir stores water; it doesn't create water. We could find ourselves paying back the loan on a deep hole. But this is no time for gloom. Under the lunar spotlight, I sing to my audience of great crested newts:

I feel the earth move under my feet
I feel my heart start to trembling...

July 20, 2006

184

A PLACE FOR THE GENUINE

MY favourite guests are those who invite themselves. It dilutes their expectations, so that even modest efforts – sweet peas in the bedrooms, new batteries in the Robert's radios – pitch the hospitality into the realm of Relais & Châteaux.

Simon and Alice are the perfect self-inviters: they only appear at breakfast and dinner, they don't complain about dog hairs, and they keep farmer's hours (disappear at 11pm). And a few days after they leave, a much-wanted book arrives. This week, it was *Collected Later Poems* of R.S. Thomas, a generous replacement for my long-lost paperback *Selected Poems*.

Now that I have this new volume (handsome, hardback, expensive), I don't know how I have lived without it. Most of the poems were written in the poet's seventies and eighties, and, like Beethoven's last quartets, they tackle the mysteries of life and death. An Anglican clergyman whose roots went deep into the earth, Thomas believed God to be Nature itself. These are poems to read during harvest, poems to read after the miracle of 2in of rain, poems to chew over after gazing at the inch-high headline on the front page of this morning's *Guardian*: 'City bonuses reach record £19bn', and its subtitle: '16% increase in payments has knock-on effect on house prices and farmland'.

Two things obsess me: poetry and the price of farmland. My shelves are full of worn, slender volumes. Penned above my desk are the lines from Marianne Moore's best-known poem, *Poetry*:

> I, too, dislike it…
> Reading it, however, with a perfect contempt for it,
>   one discovers in
> it, after all, a place for the genuine.

As for my other obsession, my study is littered with clippings, files, stacks of *Farmers Weekly* and *Farmers Guardian*, all edited around the same topic: the price of land. And here is the not-so-poetic irony: as farm incomes have plummeted, farmland prices have soared. This year saw the biggest rise since rural land surveys began 12 years ago: an increase of 7% for arable land, an increase of 11% for pasture. According to my files, the buyers are City bankers who can avoid income tax on their bonuses by buying up farmland (go figure) and Irish farmers. More than half of all land sales are to non-farmers.

Every six months, I urge my husband to write a letter

to a neighbouring farmer that begins: 'If you ever think of selling any land, we would be interested...'. It drives my husband nuts because he knows that wheat and barley won't even pay the interest*. But I suffer from 'Milton Keynes panic': that in another 10 years, this farm will be surrounded by 100,000 houses.

I confess that I'm a relict who thinks that farmers who know and love the land should farm it; that the big country house is best occcupied, Mitford-style, by bucolic squires, their wives, their enormous families, their dogs: a place for the genuine. I am also a realist. Our farm income has halved in the last decade, and we support ourselves with our farm diversification. Before my son could reverse a tractor, I was telling him that he'd have to get a job in London to afford to keep the farm.

My husband says I'm like Jeremiah, the weeping prophet who watched his nation decline. He has the kind of agricultural optimism that no genetic modification can create. I stride across fields to the rhythm of a Thomas poem:

The furies are at home
in the mirror; it is their address.

August 24, 2006

---

* See Introduction. The neighbouring farmer *did* sell... for £15,000 an acre.

SEPTEMBER SONG

MY friend Katie tells me to stop beginning my sentences with 'in my day'. She says I need a linguistic Botox. As soon as she says this, I hear every remark I make begin 'in my day'. In my day, parents didn't spend so much time parenting. Because, in my day, children weren't the centre of the universe; we were just co-residents in the family house. Parents had what Bill Bryson calls 'amicable dementia': they never quite knew what you did after school, if you did your homework, if you succumbed to peer pressure. We weren't the centre of their universe, the sun to their moon. We were just minor planets with names, and as long as nothing appeared on our report card that brought shame on the family – 'if she misses gym class one more time, she will be expelled' – life went on.

In my day, parents weren't philosophical. They didn't give us advice for a fulfilling life. They said: 'If you don't pass algebra, you'll be grounded for six weeks.' They did not say: 'All through life, you will have to do things that seem irrelevant. Learn to do them quickly and well, and then you can shove them out of sight.' They didn't say things like Nick Carraway's father in *The Great Gatsby*: 'Whenever you feel like criticising any one...just remember that all the people in this world haven't had the advantages you've had.' Which doesn't sound as profound now as it did in my day.

But times have changed, and I am never more aware of it than in September, just before taking Sam back to school. The biggest sign of change is feet. Despite the fact that all the serious newspapers have turned into magazines, with as many articles on 'the 10 best hairdryers' as on global warming, no one has written about the growth in feet sizes. Even the shoe industry hasn't kept up. Men's shoes stop at size 12. My son, aged 17, wears a size 12½, as do five of his friends. You know what they say about men with big feet: big socks. British sock sizes are size EU 41–45, equivalent to shoe size 7–11. Only at TK Maxx can I find 'Big Foot Socks', for feet size 12–14. I buy in bulk.

If I could stick to shopping, the days leading up to Sam's return to school would be idyllic. But I feel the need for meaningful heart-to-hearts while I have his undivided attention – that is to say, while he is eating a dozen oysters at Loch Fyne, one of many ritual lunches leading up to his Last Day. I tell him that in my day there were no farewell meals in restaurants. 'Were there restaurants in your day?' he asks, solemnly sipping his Muscadet *sur lie*.

189

I plough on. I tell him the story of Martin Luther King mopping the kitchen floor. Large patches hadn't even been grazed by the mop. 'Do it right,' his mother told him. 'Mop that floor as though your life depended on it.' I explain how doing even the dullest jobs well leads to greatness. Sam looks up from his oysters. 'You tell me that story every year.'

I try to lighten up. 'Never skip breakfast: it kick-starts your metabolism. Don't waste time learning the tricks of the trade: *learn the trade*. Keep your watch five minutes fast. Be kind to the new boys. Call home or I'll report your phone lost.'

This is Sam's last year at school. My days for telling him how to live a happy life are numbered. My parting shot comes from B. B. King: Nobody loves you like your Mama. And even she might be jivin'.

September 14, 2006

CIVIL WAR

YOU probably call it your belly button. Doctors tend to
call it a navel, which, despite its maritime ring, derives from
the Anglo-Saxon word 'nafe' for the hub of the wheel.
Professors of anatomy prefer the word *umbilicus*, and
describe it as the former site of attachment of the umbilical
cord. Professors of a more literary bent like the word
omphalos, the Greek word for navel, which also translates
as 'the centre of anything'. All this comes as a revelation to
me. From my first nappy change until my last, I was told
that the dimple in the middle of my tummy was 'where the
Yankee shot you'.

I never doubted it. The notion of being shot by a Yankee
was no more far-fetched to me than Adam and Eve eating
apples or Santa's sleigh holding enough toys for every child
in Mississippi. Plus, I could stick my finger in the scar, and
when I found grit there I assumed it was buckshot working
its way out. I grew up on stories of the war between the
North and the South, between Rebels and Yankees, a war

that had ended in 1865, the year my grandfather was born. My birthright was citizenship in a divided country. As the writer Lillian Smith put it: 'Beyond the mountains was the North: the land of the Damnyankees, where live People Who Cause All Of Our Trouble.'

But real as the war was to me, it wasn't called the Civil War. Although some diehards called it the War of Northern Aggression, it was mostly known as the War Between the States. Not until I was living in the North did I begin to know it as the Civil War. By then, I was surrounded by fellow students for whom the war fought between 1861 and 1865 was as remote as the American Revolution. Well-educated Yankees, they were largely unaware of the agony of a war in which six million men fought and 600,000 died, oblivious to the scars of a civil war, scars that fester, tear open, heal badly.

Perhaps that is why George Bush and Tony Blair don't want to call the war in Iraq a civil war. And who can blame them, because once the label 'civil war' is fixed to Iraq they have to swallow the rest of the truth serum, have to admit that Saddam Hussein didn't conspire with the 9/11 hijackers, had no stockpile weapons of mass destruction. Perhaps even admit that Iraq the country was invented by the British after the First World War.

One of the miracles of American history is that, after its long and tragic civil war, the Union prevailed. What has been unleashed in Iraq, the furies of ancient political, historical and cultural hatreds, makes any future 'union' impossible to envision. Seen from here, the big sky of Cromwell country, one despairs at the recklessness and stupidity that led the two countries into this war, calling it 'liberation', raising the banner of 'democracy'.

Farmers aren't historians. Our reality is nurtured in the repetition of seasons, the tyranny of weather. We read the land. The view from the plough is that we have triggered a civil war and staying will not undo what we have done. Pulling troops out slowly is nonsense: it will only make those we leave behind more vulnerable. We must leave at once. Iraq may split apart, but our presence cannot keep it together.

We will not outlive the scars of this war. A hundred years passed before the South moved on. Even now, most Southerners can come up with only one quote from William Faulkner, a quote that harks back to that war: 'The past is not dead. In fact, it's not even past.' But the past has to begin.

December 14, 2006

IV
Under The Plough

SHOPPING AND CHANGING

IT'S Martin Luther King Day and I am at Earls Court in London, wandering through the vast exhibition known as Top Drawer. This is where the nation's shopkeepers come three times a year to find things to buy for their shops.

It's Martin Luther King Day and, instead of reflecting on the brotherhood of man and justice and equality, I'm on a pilgrimage to the Mecca of upmarket materialism. I justify this in several ways. For instance, I try to support local makers, designers and producers even if the quest for 'Made in Britain' is a kind of Holy Grail of purchasing. More and more, the 'beautifully designed' and 'value for money' things are 'designed' in Britain but made in India and China. I warm to a stand of beautiful knitwear with a sign that reads 'Made in England. No thanks to Blair and Brown', because this Government has made life hell for small businesses, strangling them in red tape and legislation that makes it cheaper and easier to manufacture abroad.

Another way I rationalise my devotion to mammonistic capitalism instead of the moral reconstruction of society is that I employ 50 people. If my shop thrives (and that depends on finding good things that people want to buy), then I provide secure and flexible employment in a rural area where jobs are scarce.

My third defence is, well, I like doing it. On my first trip to Chatsworth, I fell in love with the Duchess of Devonshire's shop. In those days, she sold children's sweaters made by women on the estate from the wool of her Jacob's sheep. A table of books said 'Family', and was covered with stacks of books by Jessica, Nancy, Diana, Lord Acton. Imaginative, personal and fun, the Chatsworth shop was my inspiration when I wrestled with the challenge of diversifying a farm. And, like the Duchess, I discovered that I liked buying and selling.

And now there is a whole new world of enterprise in the countryside: farm shops, country clothing, crafts, antiques, shops attached to country houses and occupying outbuildings and tithe barns. My theory is that folks will only visit a garden or a house once a year, but if there is a great shop and restaurant they return again and again. Proof that the house and garden are a limited draw is Daylesford in Gloucestershire, which offers neither, just a series of shops, café and spa set in magnificent farm buildings. Lady Bamford, backed by JCB profits, has set a new standard: organic, local, seasonal food; exotic and beautiful things from around the world. I look at it with amazement and awe.

And yet, and yet. Deep in my heart, I believe that I should be doing more in this troubled world than encouraging people to spend, spend, spend.

Martin Luther King lived simply. Despite a love of cars, he never drove a deluxe model. He lived in modest houses. True, he liked good clothes. College friends nicknamed him Tweed because of his donnish tweed suits. After his arrest in Birmingham, Alabama, a brown bag containing his pyjamas was brought to the jail. They were made of silk.

It's Martin Luther King Day, and more than ever the world needs a leader who absolutely refuses to meet violence with violence. I place an order for 24 wool blankets made in Scotland; a dozen log baskets made in Norfolk. Like Thoreau, King believed that 'one honest man' – or woman – could morally regenerate an entire society. Now that really is a challenge to the nation's shopkeepers.

January 25, 2007

SILENT SPRING

I COME from a long line of women who achieved local fame for their ability to express their feelings at the top end of the Richter scale. I stood out from my sisterhood of snarling wolverines because I'm generally sweet-natured, which is to say I may buck and snort about war, injustice, mutant politicians and music in restaurants, but I don't tend to throw things. And by things I don't mean Waterford crystal goblets (Mama). I mean a Smith Corona typewriter flung out of a second-storey window (my sister); Darwin's *The Origin of the Species* tossed on to a bonfire (my grandmother). But if I have felt smug about my gentle spirit, I suspect my peaceful days are over. My heart now beats with the steady rhythm of rage. Or, as a character in the novel *Rat Bohemia* says: 'There is not enough anger for everything that makes me angry.'

My furies didn't begin last week so much as converge. On Monday, the 'long-awaited' United Nations report on global warming was published. The result of 2,500 scientists pooling their data, it concluded what everybody but George Bush and ExxonMobil already knew: that man has truly botched up the planet. Unless we come up with a unity of purpose greater than we've ever achieved, our children are going to pay a terrible price. Soothsayers such as James Lovelock, Al Gore and David Attenborough have been rattling pans for years, but damned if we don't keep choosing delusional leaders who think that civilisation depends on building more airport runways and giving everyone two sorts of wheelie bins.

The UN report was released on the day the first turkeys died in Suffolk. Not that we knew. Nearly a week went by before we heard the news. But by sunset on Saturday, as I shut up my birds, I knew the worst. But it wasn't the 800 dead birds and the prospect of gassing the 160,000 remaining turkeys that caused me to tremble. It was the sight of 27 long sheds stretched across the landscape, and broadcasters calling it a 'farm' in Suffolk. This is no farm, Bernard Matthews is no farmer, and the sheds housing thousands of turkeys are not 'bio-secure' units. They are havens for the development of new pandemic viruses.

I'm trying hard to focus my rage. It's too hard to be worried about everything terrible, all at once, all the time, especially in a week when more people died in Iraq than have died worldwide from avian flu. I try to make sense of this as I steam-clean the feeders for my chickens, my gaudy rare breeds, as well as for my not quite commercial flock that provides eggs with saffron-coloured yolks that we sell in the farmer's market. My birds cluck and scatter as I fill the feeders, unaware that they will be confined to their *palais de poulets* until the 'emergency' is over.

For 30 years, I've carried around my grandfather's copy of Rachel Carson's *Silent Spring*. A cotton farmer impoverished by the boll weevil, he still stood by Carson: put poison on the fields and you poison the soil; poison the soil and you poison the rivers; poison the rivers and you poison the oceans. Carson dedicated her book 'to Albert Schweitzer who said: "Man has lost the capacity to foresee and forestall. He will end by destroying the earth".'

I hope that my congenital outrage will outlast my pessimism. I latch on to a few lines in the book's introduction, from a speech by the Duke of Edinburgh in the early sixties: 'Miners use canaries to warn them of deadly gases. It might not be a bad idea if we took the same warning from the dead birds in our countryside.'

February 15, 2007

THE GREEN-EYED GIANT

HAL Crowther is one of my favourite writers. In America, he is considered to be the heir to H. L. Mencken, but for some reason he hasn't crossed the Atlantic. Maybe he's been cursed with the label 'regional' because he's a Southern writer, although that hasn't held back John Grisham.

Here's the opening of Crowther's essay 'Eating Rats at Vicksburg', from a collection called *Cathedrals of Kudzu*: 'Race is like a big crazy cousin locked in the basement, a red-eyed giant who strangled a dog and crippled a policeman the last time he got loose. We never forget that he's down there. But it's amazing how long we can ignore him, no matter how much noise he makes moaning and banging on the pipes. Our denial's almost airtight, until one day he's out in the yard again swinging a pickaxe, and all we can do is blame each other and dial 911.'

Sharp-shooting stuff, and, sitting here on a farm nine miles north of Bury St. Edmunds where I've been sowing and reaping for the past 20 years, I look at that paragraph and think: replace 'race' with 'class' and '911' with '999' and up comes a description that stretches across the land as far as the eye can see. Because even in the Britain of 2007 class is the big crazy cousin that nobody wants to talk about, but nobody truly forgets. It's all-pervasive. It's Tesco *versus* Waitrose, it's village school *vs.* pre-prep. It's toilet *vs.* loo and pardon *vs.* what? It's a film script written with a pickaxe instead of a Parker pen – I mean, of course, *The Queen*, which portrays the Duke of Edinburgh as more one-dimensional and crude than Sylvester Stallone – and it's what makes the writers of *The Archers* come up with a faux character such as Venetia – insensitive, dumb and spoiled – a caricature of 'upper-class girl'.

And it is what gave us this week, under the guise of investigative journalism, Dispatches' 'The Meddling Prince', a television programme stuffed with airy claims of 'there are fears' and 'his critics complain' and 'politicians are concerned', followed by breathtaking revelations such as comparing the price of a journey on the Royal Train with a SuperSaver ticket. In truth, when Roy Hattersley and Amanda Platell are dragged out as national interpreters of current events, it is a sure sign that the makers of the programme do not have much of a case.

To outsiders – those not to the English manor house born – the obsession with class is a depressing anachronism that cripples everyone: the resented and the resentful. It creates the insanity of a Parliament so bound up in class furies that more time is spent debating fox-hunting than the basis for entering a war whose repercussions will be felt for generations. It results in the lunacy of a programme that would lead viewers to think that Prince Charles is secretly lobbying for the Homeopathic Society to take over the country.

I wonder if the Members who voted last week believe that getting rid of the un-elected House of Lords is the first step to a classless Eden where the monarchy is silent and only travels on SuperSaver tickets. Getting rid of the monarchy (by demeaning it as a prelude to sidelining it) won't create a classless Utopia. It will only distract energy and effort from the things that really matter: education, prosperity, peace – the only things that can ever dilute the toxic waste of class.

March 22, 2007

LIST OF WISHES

OF all the injustices in this life, the one that has recently begun to pre-occupy me is this: You Can't Take It With You. Every time I make a significant purchase – a picture, a pottery jug – I have visions of it appearing on eBay for £5 next to that little 'buy it now' sign before my mourners have reached the second verse of *Amazing Grace*.

The anxiety produced by these thoughts keeps me awake at night. I gaze at my collection of Bob Dylan records and then see them tossed into the skip. I polish my Moroccan tajine dish, slightly cracked but still valuable, and hear the clash as it's dumped in the glass recycle. I look at my bound copies of *Gourmet*, 1969–1986, and hear the man in the Oxfam bookshop rejecting them.

Last week, when viewing the Bonhams' sale in the Athenaeum, I realised that I was surrounded by furniture that had been consigned to the saleroom by faithless descendants who took one look at their inheritance and said: 'Brown furniture. Let's sell.' By the bow-fronted chest of drawers I sat down and wept.

My husband is bewildered by my behaviour.

'Just update your will. That's what a codicil is for.'

Only now that reassuring word has been replaced by something called a List of Wishes, which sounds legally flimsy to me. Still, I began writing down names of godchildren, nieces, nephews and friends, and I went through the house making lists of all my treasures. The double strand of pearls with the diamond and sapphire clasp – diamonds real, sapphire glass. The amethyst earrings I wore at my wedding that need a minor repair. The rabbit-foot key ring that has brought luck to me although, alas, no luck to the original owner.

The family lawyer took one look at my 32-page List and suggested that I simplify. I took that as a hint that I should begin distributing my worldly goods now so that I could see the joy in the eyes of my beneficiaries.

I called my sister. 'Now, don't get worried. I'm fit as a fiddle but I'm doing my will. What do I have that you want?'

'Oh, lord. I don't have room for anything. I'm trying to get rid of stuff.'

'Surely I have something you want. What about Mama's diamond ring?'

'I have it already. I've had it for 10 years.'

When Sam came home for half-term, I called him into

my room. 'This is a quilt that your great-grandmother made when she was a girl. I want you to have it.'

'This is for a baby bed. It's a cot quilt. What am I going to do with it?'

'Save it for your first born.'

'I'm only 18.'

This isn't as easy as I thought, but I haven't lost heart. I'm putting tags and stickers on things, inscribing names with Indian ink. I'm not leaving anything to chance.

Last night my husband poured a whisky into a small silver tumbler. He looked underneath.

'Why does this have "Barnaby" stuck on here?'

'He's my godson.'

'But this is mine. I drink out of it every evening.'

I broke the news gently. 'I know. But you can't take it with you.'

March 29, 2007

208

REFLECTIONS FROM THE LAMBING SHED

I AM sitting in the lambing shed with a lamb tucked inside my sweater. She's having a little nap after her bottle feed of warm formula made from the yellow powder that mimics what Mother Nature produces naturally. Sadly, Mother Nature, like country life, has its share of doom and chaos, and the mother of this lamb took one look at her creation and booted her out of the fold.

Ordinarily, we deal with these displays of sheepish postnatal depression by confining ewe and lamb in a shed together and waiting for instinct to win out. With triplets, that's harder to do. It's as if a Medical Ethics Committee operates in the lambing fields, and the ewes decide to concentrate on the fittest, counting on rejection and sudden cold to be the kinder kiss of death.

Most shepherds accept this heartless Darwinian stance and, despite Defra laws, bury the lambs in fields far from the public eye. I'm the same, but more ceremonial. I line Amazon book boxes with soft, dustless straw from Mr

Dixon and sing, 'O Lamb of God, who takes away the sins of the world, have mercy upon us', as I dig little graves in the moist ground of our woodlands. But, this time, when I placed the still warm but lifeless shape in its cardboard coffin, I suddenly saw a movement, like the subtle belch of porridge on the simmer plate.

I quickly made the transition from undertaker to nursery nurse, escaping to the shed every couple of hours, bringing with me a canvas sack containing Duchy oatcakes and two Thermoses, one filled with mint tea for me, one to divide between lamb formula and the hot water bottle that has transformed the coffin into an incubator.

Like all Special Care Baby Units, this shed poses hard questions. What if this lamb survives over the next few days? Who is going to nurse it in the weeks ahead? On the Sunday after Easter, the Gospel is – or was – 'Jesus said: "I am the good shepherd: the good shepherd giveth his life for the sheep"'. As country girls, we loved this image of Jesus as a shepherd, although our livestock was limited to Jersey cows. But I also know that I fall into the category of what Jesus called the 'hireling' – meaning the people who are not committed to their task. I'm devoted and full of love for the lamb, but any day now I'll feel like going with Sam to Cambridge, eating lunch at Loch Fyne, making my pilgrimage to Kettle's Yard and second-hand bookshops.

This lamb now thinks I am her mother. She is at my mercy. I may have given her life, but she has given me a few days of peace, space where no one can find me, a quiet oasis of solitude that smells of hay and lambswool. Unlike Biblical shepherds, I haven't written psalms or named stars, but I've had time to dwell on the natural world. To remember that we are an animal species, we are part of nature. In the darkness of the lambing shed I'm more aware of the natural world, how we depend on nature for the air we breathe, the food we eat. I also have time to worry about the mess we've made of our rare and precious natural world.

These are the thoughts from the lambing shed. I only pray that I don't get distracted, don't lose interest prematurely, before the lamb is robust enough to join her cousins playing lamb games on the fallen oak tree that is their playground. This Easter I want to believe that the Lord is my shepherd and leads me forth beside the waters of comfort.

April 12, 2007

A SAVAGE KINGDOM

THE Bible Belt South has always been in awe of Virginia. When my grandfather described his mother as being 'Virginia-bred', to our ears he might as well have been saying 'our people' were kin to The Queen of England. When I made pencil rubbings of my nickels, I always started on the Monticello side, Thomas Jefferson's country house on a Virginia mountaintop. To this day, I believe that the University of Virginia at Charlottesville, founded by Jefferson in 1819, gives Oxford and Cambridge a run for its architectural money.

Before we could read, we knew the state of Virginia was named after Elizabeth I, the Virgin Queen, and that Jamestown, the desolate, marshy site of the first English settlement, was named after her successor, James I. Somewhere along the way, we also learnt that the English colonists who settled at Jamestown introduced guns to the North American continent, although we knew in our savage country hearts that the arrows of the Indians, carved from bone and stone, were faster and more accurate than the English muskets.

In fact, the principal value of the guns was to intimidate the natives. One of the written directives of the Virginia Company, the high-risk venture capitalists who put up the cash for the expedition, had been never to let novices shoot in the presence of the natives, for 'if they see your learners miss what they aim at, they will think the weapon not so terrible, and thereby will be bould to assault you'.

That nugget of historical spin wasn't taught in my history lessons. Last week, while a lone gunman made his way through a campus in Virginia, shot and killed 32 people and wounded 17 others, I was reading *Savage Kingdom: Virginia and the Founding of English America*. The book's a heart-breaking story of perilous and pestilential conditions, of bitter animosities and gruesome deaths, of meagre houses huddled together against the Indians and the weather and the unknown. The massacre by a lone student at Virginia Tech was the deadliest shooting incident by a single gunman in U.S. history.

It may be stretching the historical truth to say that America's gun problem is older than America, that it began when the English colonists took the guns out of their packing cases. But the notion of every man's right to own a gun was planted on Virginian soil from the beginning. Without the guns, the colonists couldn't have wiped out the Indians, couldn't have claimed the land and named it for a queen. They weren't carpenters or farmers or blacksmiths or cooks. Their only common skill was pulling a trigger, and they soon understood that their lives depended on it.

The next few weeks will see a shuffling of feet, a cry for greater gun control, especially as the realisation that background checks, the only gun law on the books in the U.S., aren't tough enough to prevent a massacre. Nothing life-changing or even life-saving will happen because Democrats are as scared of the gun lobby as the Republicans.

I'd like to think that Britain could show Americans what it is like to live in a country where gun ownership is tightly controlled. After Dunblane, a law was passed making handguns illegal. I reckon it's saved a lot of lives. Illegal handguns are now making parts of London like American inner cities. Whatever it is (law? politics? fear?) that makes the police hesitant to stop and search and plug the holes that allow these guns into the country, it needs to be tackled, and tackled fast. One thing that the tragedy in Virginia has proved: guns kill people.

April 26, 2007

THE LAST SPEECH DAY

SAM Greenly's mother called yesterday to ask if we had plans for Speech Day. I don't know what was going on in 1988, but most of the women who conceived boys that year named them Sam. There are three Sams in our Sam's year in his house at Harrow. I defend my naming skills by pointing out that he is the third Sam Carlisle to go to that school, the first one so long ago that his name is carved on the wall of the Old Schools, now better known as Prof Flitwick's classroom in the Harry Potter films. Tom, Jack, Max and Luke were late eighties names, too, and when my mother met Sam's friends at his third birthday party she asked me: 'How come the English name their sons after gunslingers?'

I was relieved that another Sam's mother was organising the Speech Day picnic, making it an all-inclusive affair for all the leavers in the house. Every year I suffer from what my grandmother called 'Ballroom Panic', a form of social misery that stems from not organising the picnic on time/quite right/with others. Worse than the agony of walking across a ballroom floor is the look of disappointment in your child's eyes because you still haven't cracked the picnic code.

As soon as I hung up, a blue feeling came over me. This is the Last Speech Day. The last picnic. The end of Sam's schooldays. It's not like I've been out of the room while the transformation happened, but I feel like I fell asleep. I've missed something. Worse still, I feel like I haven't told Sam everything of importance that I know. It's not just his schooldays that are coming to an end: so are my days of influencing the kind of person he will become. When I went away to school, my father wrote me a typed letter every week. Wonderful letters that covered everything from how Louis Pasteur stopped an epidemic of cholera in chickens, to the importance of reading the editorials in newspapers. He would explain how to make decent coffee, then describe watching a rooster grab a lizard and gobble it up.

Mobile phones and emails ended all that. We don't write letters that say: 'We love you, not because you get all As, but because you are decent and loving and deal with what life brings you with courage.' Instead, we write emails: 'Tennis shoes not here. Look in your cricket bag.'

Besides giving Sam a name that would not set him apart, we brought him into a world that had become gridlocked while we weren't looking. Four generations of Carlisles had gone to Harrow before our Sam, but by the time it was his turn it had become a terrifying competition, with

Common Entrance figures dangled over his head like a guillotine. The pile-up now is on the road to university. Our generation has produced a surplus of super-smart, studious, adventurous, ambitious, creative, talented, multi-lingual, much travelled *enfants terribles* who can't get into their first-choice universities despite five A levels and a gap year curing leprosy.

And then, against incredible odds, those who have looped the loops, and emerged as brainy graduates with stars and Firsts, find they are expected to work as unpaid 'interns'. Unless they are junior doctors, in which case they may not work at all.

These are not topics I'll bring up at the Speech Day picnic. I've made a vow not to rain on this parade. Instead, I'm making 144 chocolate brownies and bringing a chiller full of Wyken Moonshine, determined at last to get it right. And I know that if I call out 'Sam', a sea of manly young faces will turn my way.

May 10, 2007

THE SORROW AND THE PITY

MY favourite Jessica Mitford story dates back to her days in Washington when she was a young widow with a baby daughter. Each week she dutifully wrote to her mother, Lady Redesdale. In one letter she wrote about having tea with Lady Bird Johnson. Her mother wrote back: 'Who is this Lady Bird Johnson? I can't find them in Debrett's.'

The story came back to me this morning as I was thinking about Lady Bird Johnson's husband, Lyndon, better known as LBJ, the 36th President of the United States. I can't really say I knew him, but I once danced with him at the White House. It was at the wedding of his daughter Luci, a fellow classmate and the first girl in our class at National Cathedral School to get married. I never saw her again after her wedding. Over the years, I heard that hers was also the first divorce in our class, that she had turned into an interesting and strong-willed woman 'just like her mama'.

For the record, LBJ was one of the great presidents

of the 20th century. He was responsible for the Great Society, legislation that created Medicare (healthcare for the elderly) and Medicaid (healthcare for the poor), the only two aspects of a national health service that exists in the US. He also launched the War on Poverty, the first hope that the desolate poor living in the Mississippi Delta, the hills of Kentucky or the inner cities of Detroit and Chicago had known since Roosevelt's New Deal. Johnson, a Southerner, went further: he introduced the first civil rights legislation since 1875, passing the Civil Rights Act that achieved what the Emancipation Proclamation hadn't: equality enforceable by law.

Nobody really remembers that now. What they remember is Vietnam. In 1963, when Johnson entered the White House following the assassination of Kennedy, there were 16,000 American soldiers in Vietnam. By early 1968, there were 550,000. In 1964, Johnson was elected President in his own right by a landslide. Four years later, in a country that had turned against the war and its President, Johnson announced he would not seek re-election.

If you live long enough, you start seeing parallels in history. The next six weeks will be a Blair-a-thon, relentless analysis of the leader who brought his party into the 21st century. Here in the countryside, the lens will be aimed at the senseless slaughter of thousands of animals during the foot-and-mouth crisis, on the insanity of an urban class war fixated on fox-hunting as the bonfire of Baghdad was being laid. The more soft-hearted will try to focus his legacy on the last-minute peace in Ireland which, on the Richter Scale of Political Achievement, will be compared with Johnson's achievements in civil rights.

Looking at the endless re-runs of election night in 1997, I see the young Blairs and the happy, hopefulness of the country. I confess I was relieved that a new era was beginning. I also remember, after 9/11, my relief that this country had a leader who could articulate America's tragedy, something its own President could not do. It was that consummation of the 'special relationship' that I blamed as the war in Iraq looked increasingly inevitable, as if Mr Blair and Mr Bush had had a one-night stand and Mr Blair now faced a shotgun wedding.

In the next few weeks the pundits will be writing that we'll miss Mr Blair when he's gone. I'm not sure. When the dust of history settles, I think Mr Blair will be another Johnson: a leader who pushed his country into a futile war.

May 17, 2007

LOVE ON THE NET

Hi Sweetie, In the middle of the night, I started worrying about why Man in Augusta didn't wink back. Then I studied more closely the attributes he's looking for and saw 'someone who's spiritual but not religious'. Rufus thinks I should remove 'practising Episcopalian' from my profile because it looks like I pray before I eat.

FOR more than a year now, the Gang of Five who went through *le divorce*, and Rufus and Phoebe, her grown-up children, have been pushing Susie to join Match.com. It hasn't been easy. She thinks courtship on the internet is spooky, and when she did a scan of who's out there (you can do a 'recce' before you join), no one looked like the men in the Barbour ads, with weather-beaten faces, tweed jackets and black labradors.

Still, we told her to look on the bright side. Her cousin Betsy has just married her Match.com husband (Betsy's advice: 'If they say, "Love riding my Harley", click "delete", because that always means a man with a grey ponytail'). My cousin, Mary Faye, met her Swedish doctor online and is now Mrs Peterson. And one of our tenants, a teacher who looks like Meg Ryan, is moving to Virginia in two weeks' time to marry Stan, her PerfectMatch.com fiancé, and become step-mom to Holden and Maxwell, ages nine and seven. Stan even took his sons with him to choose the engagement ring. How *Sleepless in Seattle* is that?

Signing up on Match.com is not what anyone ever expects to do in life. Then again, no one expects to have a root canal, get arthritis, need glasses to distinguish the shampoo from the conditioner, or have your husband go off with someone who is the same age as your children. Suddenly, you have to learn how the sump pump works, how to set the thermostat on the winter boiler, how to find a lawyer who'll save your life, and how to be alone.

And once you've mastered all the above, you have to figure out how *not* to be alone. It doesn't take long to realise that friends are unreliable matchmakers. You then have three choices: dating agencies, which seem expensive and old-fashioned; personal ads, which now appear in the most highbrow magazines; and online.

The personal ads have become a cult phenomenon, pushed up a notch by Jane Juska's now immortal ad in the *New York Review Of Books*: 'Before I turn 67, I would like to have lots of sex with a man I like. If you want to talk first, Trollope works for me.' I'm waiting for the day when

Country Life gives *The Spectator* and *The Telegraph* a run for their money ('Lady Tottering lookalike, loves Elgar, Pouilly Fumé, M&S ready meals, can pluck a brace in under four minutes. House-trained dogs only need reply').

Online agencies may eclipse the personals, mainly because it's cheaper, faster and you get to see a photograph. You simply fill in a lengthy profile and then wait for a wink – or a response to your wink. Still, I'm worried that we may have pushed Susie into the wrong site. I've now learned that there are sites that narrow the field to the like-minded, such as CatholicMingle.com for Catholic singles, JDate.com (for Jewish singles); senior sites and single-parent sites. There's a lot to be said for the shortcut of familiarity. If you love the 1662 *Book of Common Prayer*, you might not want to wade through a bunch of men whose last book was *The God Delusion*. The truth is, we live in an age where it is hard to meet a soulmate. The best you can do is pray before you eat.

May 31, 2007

CONCRETE PROPOSALS

I CONFESS I've never been good with numbers. When my husband shows me the farm accounts, I get a kind of decimal cataract. My ability to fake comprehension of figures rivals Meg Ryan in *When Harry Met Sally*.

This cloud of numerical unknowing makes me quite sympathetic with the Government. When Ministers say that they expect 15,000 Poles to come here when Poland enters the EU, and then 600,000 arrive, I understand their surprise. When the cost of the Olympics leaps in four months from £4 billion to £20 billion, I can sympathise with their faulty accounting.

Still, every now and then, I hear figures that penetrate the fog. It happened this morning when I heard on the *Today* programme that the Government and British Airports Authority (BAA), the owner of Stansted, want to triple the number of flights leaving Stansted by 2015 and increase the number of passengers to 35 million a year.

To numerate innocents like myself, 35 million sounds a

lot. I had to check the papers to be sure, but there it was: 35 million passengers a year. The Government and BAA argue that expansion of the aviation industry is vital to the economy.

Numbers may be beyond my grasp, but I am sometimes praised for my common sense. So it seems obvious to me that if building a second runway at Stansted is crucial to the economic survival of the South-East, it would be foolish to stop there. It seems obvious that the time has come for England *itself* to become an airport.

The advantages are huge: by paving over all that unnecessary countryside, we could create a model of economic sustainability that would be the envy of the world. Oh the jobs we would create! China and India would hang their heads as England emerges as an economic colossus, pound notes graced with the motto *In BAA speramus.*

I'm not unaware of the downside. Next week the leader of the Inuit in Alaska is coming over here to plead against the expansion of Stansted. He will speak about the link between Britain's cheap flights and the effects of climate change on his people. It's not just polar bears that are drowning: the people who have hunted on the ice for 5,000 years are being killed by falling through the thinning ice field as they pursue their prey.

I admit that's tough, but perhaps it's time for the Inuit to get real. When all their houses fall into the sea, they can come to the land known as the United Airport Kingdom and find work in the casinos, oyster bars and Accessorise shops. In this thriving new landscape, they will soon forget the petty concerns of noise and pollution. With BAA in charge, human values (vague, unrealistic, uneconomic) will melt away faster than Arctic ice floes.

I suspect that BAA may already have plans for the United Airport Kingdom. It claims that congestion at Heathrow and Gatwick costs the economy £1.7 billion a year, whereas increasing capacity will boost it by £13 billion. That sounds like the algebraic formula for more than one runway.

In fact, I don't believe there is an alternative to turning the country into an airport. It would require a Government that honestly believes there is no connection between airport expansion and global warming. A Government that doesn't worship at the altar of Economic Growth, and its twin, the Myth of Jobs. The Government we've got 'plans to cater for 460 million passengers at UK airports by 2020'.

I may not shine at pure maths, but I can recognise a civilisation floating on thin ice.

June 7, 2007

DRIVING ON THE RIGHT

ON my 15th birthday, I drove my mother's Corvair to the courthouse in Magnolia, Mississippi, to get my driving licence. I got everything right on the written test except for the blinking yellow light. I ticked 'Stop' instead of 'Slow down, proceed with caution'. Then I went to the sheriff's office to take the driving test.

'Honey, I don't reckon your daddy would've let you come down here if you didn't know how to drive,' Sheriff Guy said. With that, he signed the form and I got my first driving licence.

I've told the story so often I now sound like Sheriff Guy himself. If my audience is appreciative, I follow it up with the story of my British driving licence. For years, I drove in England with a French licence and a Maryland licence, long past the legal time limit. Then something awful happened. My husband was made Minister for Roads and Traffic. 'Oh lord,' I groaned, 'I'd better get my British licence now.' 'No,' he said softly. 'You'll never pass. You'll have to wait until I'm no longer there.' The day he shuffled out of the Department of Transport, I signed up for driving lessons to brush up for my test.

Those lessons were a revelation. Although I could top up the radiator and change a tyre, I only looked in the rear-view mirror to put on eyeliner. I could have driven from London to Kathmandu without looking back. On rare occasions when I did, I saw drivers shaking their fists in rage because I was blithely hogging the fast lane.

Those stories don't seem so funny to me now. I've deleted tales of driving on the farm, age 13, from my redneck repertoire. I've asked my husband to stop telling how his sister, age 17, drove him and his twin sister, age 15, from London to Spain (mind you, she was Christabel Carlisle, a racing driver of some renown). When you have a son learning to drive, all these stories feel like a flat tyre.

Lamp posts swathed in flowers, roadside memorials, tell another story. Car crashes are the leading cause of death among 15- to 20-year-olds in this country. In the past four years, the death rate among young drivers has doubled. Every hour, a person under 25 is killed or seriously injured in a car accident.

We spend a fortune, emotional and financial, making sure our sons and daughters are stuffed with A levels and decent manners. We celebrate rites of passage, including one at 17: the inalienable right to drive a car if you pass a test that doesn't require you to know how to drive on a motorway, drive in a storm/at night/with three friends in the car. Every flower-draped lamp post makes me think that a year of lessons teaching teenagers how to drive safely for the rest of their lives is more useful a curriculum than a year devoted to Philip II of Spain.

Which is why I'm signing my son up with a company called a2om (stands for Alpha to Omega Motoring) for driving lessons that are aimed at young boys and their anxious parents. The founder, Nick Rowley, has created an enlightened curriculum that uses neuroscience to accelerate the development of the frontal lobe, that vital part of the brain that can anticipate risk and doesn't fully develop until you're 24. A friend's son admits: 'It's the Oxbridge of driving instruction.'

Sam insists that the a2om course isn't necessary, that he already knows it all, but I'm with Sheriff Guy on this one: I don't reckon he's getting the car keys until his frontal lobe is the size of a watermelon.

June 28, 2007

WHEN GOVERNMENT WAS GOOD

ALTHOUGH I don't budge, my day begins at 5:30am with *Farming Today*. I remember when it was a Balzacian account of rural life, complete with the market prices of feeder cattle, lean hogs, pork bellies and Cornish daffodils. Now it focuses on EU legislation, epic flooding, fruit crops lost, feral hogs, dying bees, pestilence and plague. I wake up every morning in the Old Testament.

By the time the *Today* programme takes over, I'm drifting back to sleep. It takes a seismic blast to penetrate the fog, such as James Naughtie's interview with Jimmy Carter a few weeks ago. Mr Naughtie asked the 39th President of the United States how, in the twilight of Tony Blair's premiership, he would judge the Prime Minister's support of George Bush. An audible pause preceded Carter's reply: 'Abominable. Loyal... blind. Apparently subservient. I think the almost undeviating support of Great Britain for the ill-advised policies of President Bush in Iraq has been a major tragedy for the world.' It was the word 'subservient' that woke me up. It's the word I've been trying to think of for the past four years.

I don't think Oxford University decided to bestow an honorary doctorate on Mr Carter last week based on that interview because these things take years to plan. But the remarks added lustre to the occasion. By the time the 82-year-old youthful President stood up to address his audience, the frenzy of devotion in The Sheldonian felt more like First Ebenezer Church. But Jimmy Carter is no ordinary former president. He is a rare politician who believes that the priority of politics is justice.

I confess I have a soft spot for Mr Carter. Not because he was a farmer who made it to the White House, but because every morning he was there he listened to half an hour of Mozart or Beethoven. He's in the history books as the only president who ever went to New York's Metropolitan Opera House. The opera that evening was *Aida*.

And I get touchy when he's called a religious fanatic. The most truly Jeffersonian president since Jefferson, he held firmly to the separation of Church and State. Unlike all his successors, Carter never held a prayer service in the White House.

I get touchier still when Carter is called 'the best ex-President'. True, his achievements since he left office are impressive – 27 books, Habitat for Humanity, a long war against deadly diseases in Africa, the monitoring of dubious elections around the world. But his achievements as President weren't small: the peace agreement between Egypt and Israel that has lasted unbroken for 28 years. The Panama Canal treaties. Relations with China. The foundation for the Holocaust Memorial Museum in Washington. The first energy policy. Millions of acres of Alaskan wilderness preserved as a national park.

In the Sheldonian, the young men, some with their academic gowns still slung over their shoulders, looked so young. They weren't even born when this man was President. Now, they are 'draft age'. When Mr Carter was elected, the war in Vietnam had ended, but wounds were still raw. The day after he entered the White House, Mr Carter granted amnesty to the young men who had dodged or evaded the draft. He believed that only when the hundreds of thousands of America's young men could come back home would the country begin to heal. It wasn't a political decision; it was a moral commitment. And now that's history.

July 5, 2007

OUR GREAT DAME

FRIENDS in Maine tell of opening a closet in a large summer house and finding two boxes. One box is labelled 'String'; the other 'String Too Short To Save'. That phrase echoes because my mind is stuffed with bits of string that I save for the day I will braid it into ropes of understanding. I've been fiddling with string like that for the past few weeks, ever since a family party to celebrate the 80th birthday of my husband's much-loved aunt.

For most of the years I've known Anne, she's lived on her own – she and her husband, Donald, were divorced in 1959 – and she's been a model for how to be alone. She's balanced the productive solitude required for her life as a scientist with the undistracted, happy time spent with her family and friends. She's lived a life of material modesty that's caused wonder to us all, the only element of lavishness the holidays with her children, their spouses and her grandchildren: skiing each winter, summers in countries requiring complicated visas. These sojourns usually included her former husband – and father of her three children – and his wife, a tight-knit, brainy and congenial tribe that left their cousins envious and amazed.

A couple of years ago, after Donald was widowed, he and Anne bought a house together in north London a 10-minute walk from their two daughters. The top floor is Anne's; the first floor with its kitchen and sitting room is the communal space; and the ground floor is Donald's, including a study for his vast library. We all find this Life Comes Full Circle arrangement touching, not because it's 'civilised', but because it is an affirmation of half a century of mutual respect, love, friendship and intellectual collaboration.

Anne McLaren and Donald Michie began their married life as young scientists researching the effect of the maternal environment on mice, seeking to untangle the mystery of Nature *versus* Nurture. Over the years, Donald moved into the field of computers and artificial intelligence, work inspired by his wartime job as a codebreaker at Bletchley. Anne stayed with her mice. In an early experiment, she cultured mouse embryos in a test tube and placed them in the uterus of a surrogate mother. Live baby mice – and the miracle of IVF – were born.

The notion that 'in dreams begin responsibilities' was felt acutely by Anne, and she combined her research in the laboratory with her demanding work on the Warnock Committee, laying the basis for the Human Fertilisation and Embryology Act. Although she described herself as an ethical ignoramus, she was calm and lucid on the ethics of embryo research – and, more recently, embryonic stem cell research. Calm and modest, a fellow of the Royal Society (she was elected Foreign Secretary, its first female officer) and a Dame. Close friends and members of her family were always the last to know her news.

Until last Saturday. Within hours, we learned that Anne and Donald had died together in a car accident on the M11, driving from Cambridge to London. All week long, we've struggled to be philosophical. They both would have hated the loss of energy and of enchantment, hated the hidden darkness of a broken old age. We tell ourselves that, as a geneticist, Anne always looked at life appreciatively, never dictatorially or sceptically. And reading the full-page obituaries, we remember Anne's great legacy: she had the vision and the patience to turn string too short to save into the science that creates life.

July 19, 2007

THE CHINA SYNDROME

MY decision to bypass the 4th of July until the troops come home left us feeling a little flat. The Weber barbecue stayed rusting in the game larder like a piece of redundant farm machinery. The vine prunings for pan-smoking turned to tumbleweed. I figured before things got worse we'd better have a party, so I announced that we'd celebrate Thoreau's birthday.

When all I owned was a VW van, Thoreau's essay *Civil Disobedience* was my rallying cry. Now that I have a few acres, it's *Walden* that stirs my soul. He began writing the book *Walden Pond* when he was 27 years old, determined to 'Simplify, simplify, simplify... to live deliberately, to front only the essential facts of life'.

I told my family the theme of our Thoreau Party would be 'Simplify'. All the food would come from the garden, the fields, the woods, the vineyard. My husband quickly poured a whisky (road miles: 400). 'Your idea of simplifying is to buy online from The White Company,' said Sam.

Undiscouraged, I put on my Flax apron and went out to dig the early potatoes. The first essential fact I fronted was blight. I dug them up anyhow. Still, Sam's observation niggled. White sheets flapping on the line make me feel almost Amish. It was one of those 'The Gift to Be Simple' moments that led me to buy toothpaste at Marks & Spencer, seduced by the plain all-white tube with 'Protect' written in pale grey letters. I felt pure and simple until I read the fine print on the back.

It's not the diethylene glycol, an ingredient in antifreeze found in toothpastes from China sold in the US that puts me off. Not even the deaths of 51 people in Panama now blamed on Chinese-made cough syrup tainted with the same chemical. What drives me *crazy* is that M&S thinks I want my toothpaste made in China.

I don't know why I was surprised. I live in a little corner of England that is becoming forever China: 50 minutes from Felixstowe Docks, a vast dockscape of cranes (all made in China) lit up like Coney Island. Every day, 22,000 containers arrive here from China, loaded with iPods, televisions, pet food, tyres, North Sea fish (caught here, processed in China), soft toys, trainers, cashmere sweaters, Waterford crystal, Wedgwood china, tennis rackets and toothpaste. Waiting lorries hook up with these containers before heaving themselves on to the A14, a road that requires nerves of steel from mere car drivers. Every 10th vehicle is a lorry with a container marked China Ocean

Shipping Company, or COSCO, the Chinese shipping line whose vessels are 1,000ft long and carry 9,500 containers.

It now takes just 22 days for these container ships to get from China to Felixstowe. This year, eight million containers arrived. We don't produce anything the Chinese want, so they returned empty. By 2025, 14 million containers a year are predicted.

Although I am writing this on an iMac made in China, I'd like to slow down these boats. It won't be easy. Even when I think I'm buying stuff made in Scotland, Ireland, England, I often find that it is designed here but made in China.

It's all happened so fast. First, everything got cheaper: clothes, computers. We all got more and more stuff. Heck, we never had it so good. And before we knew it, primary schools were offering our children lessons in Mandarin as if their lives depended on it.

Instead of fireworks on Thoreau Day (99 percent of all fireworks in the UK come from China), I lit a candle. A candle made in Cornwall. Call it a candle blowing in the wind.

July 26, 2007

GREEN LITE

EVER since I read Nick Hornby's *About a Boy*, in which the hero measures his coolness quotient, I've kept a little inventory of my own cool status. For instance, I'm sitting here in Nicole Farhi grey flannel trousers (5pts). The top button doesn't do up (deduct 5pts). I saw the new film *2 Days in Paris* in Paris (5pts). The French was so fast I needed subtitles (deduct 5pts).

Actually, now that Green is the new 'cool' I've been scoring higher. When you live in the country, it's easier to be Green than cool. For example, we have a farmer's market here on the farm every week, nestled in the old sheep pens (10pts). Every other Friday, I go to Waitrose and buy hunks of Parmigiano Reggiano, Lavazza coffee, Puy lentils (deduct 5pts). We have our own vineyard which dramatically cuts down on road, sea and air miles (10pts). Each evening, I yearn for a glass of ForestVille Merlot from California (deduct 10pts plus 5pts off because Merlot is now uncool).

If this sounds 'Green lite', I can do better. I know Al Gore (100pts). I haven't seen him since we were in the Religious Club together at school (deduct 50pts). I voted for him seven years ago (10pts). It didn't count (incalculable). Last Christmas, we watched *An Inconvenient Truth* instead of *It's a Wonderful Life* (5pts). My family called it 'How Al Grinch Stole Christmas' (deduct 10pts).

Still, I've soldiered on: I've banned plastic bags from Wyken despite complaints from customers. My house is a bottled water-free zone. But, frankly, I'm beginning to lose heart. It's not just all those stories about a new coal mine opening in China every 48 hours, nor even the voice of David Attenborough pointing out that as the ancient sea turtle deposits her doomed eggs in the sand a chemical plant is being built 100 yards away. No, what has me feeling forlorn is the way the movement has been hijacked by self-righteous politicians hell bent on legislation that won't save a single polar bear.

Believe me, I'm happy for energy-guzzling lightbulbs to be phased out, but I'm terrified that when the 2011 deadline comes (which also outlaws all lights on dimmer switches) dolphin-friendly folk like me will be left sitting in the dark, the twilight of our lives spent in the twilight of energy-efficient lightbulbs.

Reading in bed is one of my great joys in life, followed by my first cup of coffee in the morning. I grind my beans. I boil my (filtered) water. I make my organic, Fairtrade, shade-grown, bird-friendly coffee in a glass Chemex coffee pot using unbleached filter papers. I then add Jane Capon's organic Jersey milk. So imagine my surprise at Defra wanting consumers to switch to UHT milk to reduce greenhouse-gas emissions so that by 2020 90 percent of milk on sale in the UK will not require refrigeration.

I may not be Everywoman, but I feel the inner tremors of a backlash. Not wacky 'global warming is a myth' tremors, but 'governments expanding airports/starving public transport/building thousands of new digital-television towers' tremors. As soon as governments stop causing the ecological crisis, I'll drink old milk and sit in the dark.

Meanwhile, I'm designing a refuge where I can escape the fundamentalist rhetoric of Green politicians. I think Kevin McCloud will approve. The outer walls are made from volumes of *Hansard* 1979–1997, the inner walls from copies of COUNTRY LIFE 1996–2007. The insulation is by vintage Nicole Farhi, size 10s and 12s.

October 25, 2007

FOR RICHER AND RICHER

ALTHOUGH I was brought up with the mantra 'it's just as easy to fall in love with a rich man as a poor man', I didn't really believe it. The richest men in our rural landscape tended to be car dealers who didn't spark the romantic imagination. All the same, the message must have lodged in my unconscious, because the day came when I fell in love with a millionaire.

Not that you would know it. I married the kind of Englishman who hides his worth under a bushel along with any sign of worldly wealth. His wardrobe consists of his grandfather's smoking jacket, an old overcoat that Sybille Bedford asked me to drop off for her at the Red Cross shop, a pair of Bally shoes that Robert Carrier left behind when he left England. He has tweeds that belonged to the cousin who bought Wyken in 1920, and drives an unreliable Freelander with a book value of £250. In fact, I would never know I was married to a millionaire if I didn't read *Farmers Guardian* each week, nervously tracking the price of farmland. You probably know where this is heading: farmland has never been higher (£4,000 per acre), and we are only millionaires if we sell the farm. In the Deep South, this is called 'land poor' – lots of land and no money in the bank.

Still, 'millionaire' makes me think of novels by F. Scott Fitzgerald, crocodile shoes and fur coats with initials sewn in silk thread in an italic script. I never believed that it would become so ordinary. To paraphrase W. H. Auden, now even a hat rack can be a millionaire; all he needs is a three-room flat in London. Nowadays, if the Great Gatsby wants to be so rich it makes Daisy cry, or make *The Sunday Times* Rich List, he has to be a billionaire, as in Russian oligarchs; as in the Bank of England bailing out Northern Rock to the tune of billions; as in £9.3 billion and rising for the London Olympics.

When 'billion' began to become common currency, it triggered one of those linguistic issues that can lead to delirium. In America, a billion is 1,000 million and it's written 1,000,000,000. In Britain, a billion is a million million, written 1,000,000,000,000. But in a scene straight out of *Bremner, Bird and Fortune*, the British Government decided the Special Relationship was doomed if we couldn't agree on the Billion Thing. Britain promptly dropped three zeros. Which has probably saved everyone a lot of money. For instance, the Bank of England has bailed out Northern Rock to the tune of £23 billion so far, which is £730 for every taxpayer in the UK. There are 6.6 billion people in the world. That's about £3.38 for every person on earth.

I always prided myself on my numerical illiteracy until I heard that, after the Paddington rail crash, John Prescott was asked how much a new braking system would cost. 'A million. A billion. I don't care,' he replied. This shocked Andrew Dilnot, the fiscally passionate Pro-Vice-Chancellor of Oxford, who said Mr Prescott *should* care because 'a million seconds is 11 days. A billion seconds is 32 years'.

I admit I find my new numeracy quite exciting. I twitch when I hear a barrel of oil costs $100, but I take comfort that the price of wheat has gone up 100% in the past two years (from £60 to £120–£130 a ton). We aim to average four tons or 140 bushels per acre, and this year I'm planting a variety called Einstein. Just think: a billion hours ago, our ancestors were living in the Stone Age, advising their daughters to fall in love with a rich man.

November 15, 2007

THE TREADMILL OF REGRET

LAST week, I went through three years of Christmas cards. It says something about my acceptance of clutter that the three baskets (2004, 2005 and 2006) were stored beneath a table in the passage that I walk along 100 times a day.

Still, it's a good Advent job, a time of spiritual preparation which also means tracking down the window cleaner and the chimney sweep, bringing the first paper whites into the house, a subliminal acting out of the Collect for the four short weeks, when we entreat God to 'give us grace that we may cast away the works of darkness...'.

Near the bottom of the 2006 basket, I found a card written in familiar, tiny handwriting, with the portrait of Doris Lessing by Leonard McComb that hangs in the National Portrait Gallery. The description of the picture was in language as fresh and clear as the portrait itself, a present from Sister Wendy Beckett, nun, art critic, friend, Consecrated Virgin and hermit. The last two terms have specific meaning in her Catholic world, referring to her chaste devotion to God and the caravan in which she lives in solitary contemplation at the Carmelite Monastery in Quidenham, Norfolk.

Advent is also the time when I mend patches of neglect. I gazed guiltily at Sister Wendy's letter, then remembered that she thinks guilt is self-indulgent and ego-fixated. She prefers contrition, which moves you forward. I promptly sent a contrite email to Amanda, our go-between, who gets in touch with Sister Wendy and arranges to collect her and bring her here to lunch.

This isn't easy. Sister Wendy only leaves her solitary life if it is to do something 'useful', something that will generate income for the monastery. I organise a book signing of her two most recent books: a collection of her favourite 100 poems, and *Sister Wendy on Prayer*, her most personal book.

As soon as she enters the restaurant, the eyes of fellow diners open wide in recognition and surprise. No one expects to see a nun dressed in full habit here, but her black cloak looks at home nestled among the Barbours on the coat rack. Over the years, I've asked Sister Wendy all the questions you long to ask a nun. Yes, she loves wearing a habit – 'it simplifies life'; and, yes, she shaves her head – 'so much easier'.

She only ever wanted to be a nun. She became a novice at 16; and, two years later, 'because I couldn't cook or sew, being so very untalented, I was sent to Oxford'. She read

English at St. Anne's and emerged with a Congratulatory First. A scholar and a reader (she loves Jane Austen, Henry James, Agatha Christie), she is as open-minded as she is open-hearted: she believes that her Church will eventually accept contraception; she thinks priests should be able to marry; she is all for gay partnerships.

An aura of holiness and happiness surrounds her, but everyday life intrudes. Despite repeated promises from her publishers, only half the books arrive. Plus, she has a painful cough, caught in Kiev last week where she went to look at one of the eight surviving pre-iconoclastic images of the Madonna. She is worried because next week she flies to Texas to deliver a lecture at the Kimbell Museum. At 77, she doesn't feel inclined to slow down.

As the wine arrives, I begin to apologise for my neglect, to explain my Advent vow. She begins to fish into the deep folds of her habit and presents me with a collection of meditations on Advent she has made just for me. In a gentle voice, she suggests a different vow: 'Jump off the treadmill of regret, my dear.' With that reprieve, we toast to 'Advent' because, truly, the wait is worth it.

November 29, 2007

COMFORT AND JOY

I FIRST heard Handel's *Messiah* during the war in Vietnam. The senior girls were allowed to attend a rehearsal for a performance in the National Cathedral that was given the following evening for the Great and the Good of Washington DC. As we filed in, we were given a sheet of paper fresh from the Ditto machine. I inhaled the perfume of the purple ink as I read the titles of the 54 movements, a kind of Reader's Digest condensed life of Christ, sung in the familiar and majestic language of the King James Bible.

My memory of that performance is of feeling as though my life had just begun, that I was hearing trumpets, timpani, violins and human voices for the first time. When everyone leapt to their feet for the 'Hallelujah!' chorus, I felt alive with joy. I also thought it was the end, and I was baffled when the soprano started singing again.

A lot happens in the *Messiah*, and truly there are no boring bits; but, even now, nearly four decades later, I suspect I still managed to think about other things. I probably thought about my sister who was getting married a few weeks later, a large Christmas wedding that I dreaded. (Years later, I learned that she had dreaded it, too.) I may have worried about my Uncle Jack, a helicopter pilot in Vietnam, and about my cousin Steve who was about to go there, or perhaps I only thought about myself: university applications, a pair of boots I wanted, a boy I liked. Although I've travelled far and wide to hear a Bach *Mass* or a Mozart *Requiem*, I date my habit of thinking about life while listening to great music to that first performance of the *Messiah*.

I begin every concert with a vow to concentrate, to focus on the melodic shape, to follow the harmonic structure, simply to *listen* to the music. Sitting in the cathedral in Bury St Edmunds last night, listening to a beautiful performance of the *Messiah*, I made it through the Old Testament prophecies and reached the New Testament birth of Jesus before my thoughts began to wander.

It wasn't a profound distraction, not thoughts of war and peace, but of tree lights. Earlier in the week, my friend Katy told me to replace my incandescent Christmas lights with LEDs (light emitting diodes). 'Ten strands of incandescent lights, left on from dusk till midnight, produce up to 300lb of CO_2. Long-lasting LEDs produce a mere 30lb.' I was torn: buy all new lights for the sake of the planet but dump the old lights in a landfill? I pushed myself back into the music, yearning for the spiritual certainty of the 'Hallelujah!' chorus.

I used to believe that the *Messiah* was best performed in a liturgical slow time, not during the hurly-burly of Christmas. Handel didn't even write it for Christmas – it was first performed in Dublin in April 1742. But now I think that the great oratorio is a perfect starting point for Christmas. As the lights dim, I enter the spirit of the music, the birth of Jesus, which is the beginning of the Christian faith. Other thoughts scatter in and out – menus, presents, sheets. And sadder thoughts: three funerals in the past month, three families whose worlds have been torn asunder, their first Christmas in a time of grief. But the music is comfort and joy, and it moves me closer to the miracle of Christmas.

As the pure soprano voice sings, I say the silent prayer I always say during the *Messiah*: let this be the Christmas that I give the only gifts that matter, peaceful surroundings and my undivided attention.

December 20, 2007

V
Seed Corn

THRIFT OR RE-GIFT

AS soon as we made the pact, I had the feeling that it was like writing a suicide note. This was the agreement: 'children only' Christmas presents. No presents for grown-ups. I saw it as a noble stand against rampant consumerism. I felt virtuous, relaxed and relieved. Only one thought weighed heavily: if everyone took such a high moral stand, my own shop would go out of business and we would die poor and lonely.

It seemed to be the mood throughout the land. My friend Susie's family version of the pact was Thrift or Re-Gift. This translates as everything has to come from a charity shop or be something you already own. Note: these pacts do not extend to anyone under the age of 21, unless the recipients are the tousle-headed boys in the Piaget watch ads or daughters eyeing their grandmother's fifties Chanel suits.

Despite cries of Scroogeness, this form of home shopping can be tender and creative. Susie's cousin Portia gave her an ancient Brooks Brothers' box carefully tied with string. Inside were three tiny sweaters Susie had knitted for her two babies, Phoebe and Rufus, and then passed on to Portia's babies. Portia had saved them for nearly 30 years and returned them to Susie on the eve of Rufus's engagement to Maura.

Portia is one of life's good givers. On Susie and Tom's 25th wedding anniversary, she disappeared upstairs before dessert and re-emerged wearing the bridesmaid's dress she'd worn a quarter of a century earlier. She couldn't zip it up, but she'd saved it all those years to give to Susie's daughter.

I don't know if the art of giving is Nature or Nurture. Now that an autopsy can identify a musician by the shape of the brain, it's just a matter of time before they'll be able to distinguish between the naturally generous and the tight-wad brain. Most people are a little of both. My mother-in-law wrote lavish cheques to her grateful grandchildren, but she would not willingly wander through shops looking for the perfect present. This may have been a legacy of the war years. My husband tells how he and his sisters opened all their toys on Christmas morning, but by evening the toys had vanished, wrapped up and put in the attic where they remained until the following year.

Lingering frugality may also explain why my mother-in-law didn't like to receive lots of presents. She began the New Year by putting most of her presents into her Present Drawer. Occasionally, she got muddled and returned the

Liberty scarf/lavender pillow/Diorissimo *eau de toilette* to the original giver. Feelings were hurt, but the damage rarely lasted more than a decade.

One unexpected bonus of the Christmas pact is that I felt less guilty about giving myself presents. This year, I bought a Magimix kettle from Peter Jones and a lamp from Nicky Haslam's shop on Ebury Street that looks like it was made by Diego Giacometti for the Picasso museum. I paid for these treasures with the Krugerrand my husband has given me for the past nine Christmases. On Boxing Day, he puts the hefty gold piece back in the gun safe (a wartime memory?) for another year. But early in December I slipped off to Spink's and generously converted my piece of gold into something more satisfying.

Every New Year, I vow to conquer my materialism and live a simpler, spiritual life. This year I will have a head start because I've parted with things I no longer want or need. It is very satisfying to begin the year in the rich glow of my new lamp, although the Present Drawer looks worryingly bare.

January 3, 2008

OPTIMISM FOR BEGINNERS

ON the scale of New Age consciousness, I barely register. I know that I am a Leo, my husband is an Aries and my son is an Aquarian, but I don't believe anything is written in the stars. When I hear someone say, 'When your time is up, your time is up', I cringe. I use the words 'fate' and 'destiny' with the same nervous caution I use 'brilliant'. Still, when I saw the barn owl flying low on the Walsham Road, leading me all the way home, I thought it was a sign.

Not that I could decipher the sign. I was too terrified that this rare and beautiful creature was on a cataclysmic journey, that he would be hit by an oncoming car even as he guided me home. When he turned towards Stowlangtoft, I followed him, although it was not in the direction I was going. By now, I had my warning lights on, Maria Callas was singing the aria from *Turandot* on Classic FM, and all I wanted in the world was for this owl to survive. At last, he flew into the carved hollow of a dead oak tree on the side of the road. I stopped the car and stared at him. He stared back. I tried to pass thought waves, a kind of inter-species morphic resonance: *be careful.* He looked back at me, his head cocked like a Christmas card owl, as if to say: why is this woman in a Volvo stalking me?

When I got home, I told my husband that I thought the owl was flying low because he was a youngster, just discovering the power of flight. My husband, a true countryman, explained that he was flying low because he was searching for prey along the hedgerows. He has seen my owl on walks, and he too worries about cars.

'The owls will fare better when all the six-metre margins on the fields have grown up,' he tells me. But I am not hopeful about the future. I keep thinking about Barn Owl Fate, the kind of fate that isn't decreed by some cosmic crossroad but is the inevitable consequence of a pile-up of circumstances.

My son calls my view on life 'Mama's Fatalism'. I call it the New Realism. When he saw that I'd bought a book of poems by Sophie Hannah called *Pessimism for Beginners*, he said, 'Surely you're ready for *The Advanced Pessimist*'. That reaction caused a small epiphany, all the more appropriate as the season begins.

It is a beautiful word, Epiphany, Greek for 'something made clear'. Not that it is easy to see what is being made clear in an age of suicide bombers, climate change, knife crime and house repossessions. I could go on. But what if the barn owl is a sign of something made clear? What if these precious creatures are coming back and this time we will treasure them. That the wars of today will make us wary of future wars? That the climate change that threatens us all also unites us all? That the underbelly of the global climactic catastrophe is recognising our common humanity?

The book I'd like to write this year would be called *Optimism for Beginners*. This slim volume would contain unsentimental readings for the shaky, the wary and the gloomy. It would advise readers to begin with a 30-day moratorium of newspapers, radio and television. The book wouldn't be found in bookshops under 'religious writings', but it would begin with the Epiphany reading where Paul calls us to be 'transformed by the renewing of our minds'. On the cover would be a barn owl, soaring majestically and securely above the cars.

January 10, 2008

FAREWELL TO ST JAMES'S SQUARE

ONCE upon a time, I was a passionate joiner. An investigation into my past would reveal that I once belonged to SNCC (Student Nonviolent Coordinating Committee) and the Peace and Freedom Party. I was also a member of the Oil, Chemical and Atomic Workers Union where I rose to become a shop steward. But when I left my radical past behind, I also surrendered the desire to belong to anything. Until I came to England to write about the 19th-century Romantics. To prepare for this task, I joined a unique institution. The day I became a card-carrying member of the London Library (No 01045) in St James's Square was one of the happiest of my life.

Unlike earlier memberships, there were no meetings. No one examined the books I read for signs of bourgeois feminism (a bad thing) or infantile individualism (ditto). Once a week, accompanied by Adam, my philosophical labrador, and a briefcase stuffed with pens, paper, Bonio and water bowl, I drove from Putney to St James's Square, where we would spend the day in the Library, me high up in the hinterlands, with Goethe, Novalis, Byron and Shelley, Adam stretched out in the entrance beneath the hats and coats. Sometimes, Adam's inner alarm would go off and he'd come looking for me. Staff were afraid that a dog paw might get stuck in the open grilles of the walkways, and suddenly I would hear a desperate whisper: 'Hello? Are you there? Adam's searching for you!'

But the day came when I left the city and moved to the country. Adam was relieved, but I missed the London Library. I missed the smell of books, the first-floor reading room, the portraits on the stairs, especially the historian Thomas Carlyle, the Library's founder and the link between the last Romantics and Victorian culture. Despite no reduced rate for country members I stayed a faithful member. Some years I didn't borrow a single book. Like friends who describe themselves as cultural Jews, I became a cultural intellectual, the kind who reads the reviews but not the books; the ersatz scholar who subsidises the genuine scholar.

In front of me is a reminder that my membership is due for renewal on February 1. The letter sits in my London Library file, fat with information about the new rate increase, an 80% jump from £210 to £375 a year. A letter from Sir Tom Stoppard, the Library's president, defends the move. Another informs me that married couples who are both members qualify for an annual reduction of £25 each. The scholar under the age of 25 can purchase life membership for £16,000. For the dreamy optimist aged 70, life membership is £3,200.

Gazing at these figures, my heart sinks. This is what happens when people with no commercial verve start running great institutions. Instead of thinking creatively – for instance, how to double the membership from 8,000 to 16,000 and make this place genuinely viable – they decide to raise the present fee, as if the London Library is a slightly shabby but exclusive club in St. James's. How much more imaginative to offer life membership after the age of 60 for £1,000, thereby attracting 1,000 new members.

I once dreamt of publishing a slender volume in which I gratefully acknowledge the 'staff of the London Library'. I now feel it's time to tighten the belt and surrender my intellectual vanity together with my membership. The London Library will join the list of places I've done and things I've been.

January 24, 2008

LETTER FROM PARIS

FROM my window, I look out on to the fountain of the rue Mouffetard, a café that serves a decent *croque madame*, a municipal bicycle rank and L'église St-Médard, the church where Jean Valjean accidentally encounters Javert in *Les Misérables*. Like most Paris churches, its churchyard is now a children's playground, making it a living part of the neighbourhood.

I also have a nice patch of sky, what Paris estate agents call a *'vue sans vis à vis'*. It's a scene that could be straight out of a film starring Jean Gabin. Rather, it could have been until three days ago, when I watched a platoon of men in Day-Glo vests install a tall double street light with space-age round globes enclosing yellow sodium lights. A view as timeless as a novel by Colette, as exquisite as a suit by Chanel, has been redesigned by visionary vandals.

I'm a Francophile who doesn't share the English preference for the French countryside. Keep the sun, the heat, the smell of rosemary and eucalyptus. My *nostalgie de la boue* is triggered by the smell of chestnuts on street corners, Paris buses whose routes are as fixed as the river that divides the city, a *carnet* of Métro tickets that makes me feel like I've won the lottery.

This wintry *séjour* began with Sam's gap year, a scheme I surrendered to more than embraced. When he proposed a course at the Sorbonne, I immediately said, 'Oui'. When he balked at living with a French family, I even said, 'Si'. But as I studied the rentals page in the *New York Review of Books*, I began to think, 'Me!'. Soon, I was corresponding by email with a Yale professor with a flat in the 5th *arrondissement* and negotiating with Sam: I'll rent a flat for a month and you can stay with me while you look for a place of your own. He agreed, despite a card from his cousin with a photograph of a middle-aged matron and the message: 'What's wrong with your mother coming with you on your gap year?'

In fact, Sam is travelling and I've had the flat to myself. Each day, I wake up to a rainy Paris until I remember that they wash the streets every morning. It's easy to get confused, because most days the City of Light is grey and I feel like another American who lived in Paris, Edith Wharton, whose biographer Hermione Lee observed: 'Happiness makes her sad.' Lovers of Paris bring their idealism and nostalgia with them and cannot bear the changes that the *indigènes* hardly notice. If only the Parisians objected to the street lights that make apartment life after 5pm feel like life in a police line-up. If only Parisians objected to the even greater horror of loudspeakers attached to the street posts. On market days, a medley of Bill Haley and the Comets and low prices for tripe *saucisson* blasts the *quartier* in stereo.

'Ah,' friends say, 'at least the cafés and restaurants are no longer a thick haze of Gauloises!' But who could have predicted that a side effect would be that the Parisians have asserted their ancient *droit de pavé*. The fuming clientele now dress like bears and sit outside the cafés with their cigarettes day and night. The outdoor life has liberated their Gallic essence, and they now speak as if they're on stage. I learned the phrase for ear plugs (*quies boules*) as the *pharmacien* confided that, since the ban started on January 1, he's sold 90 pairs.

A gap month in Paris is like meeting up with an old lover: you're judgemental, eager to convince yourself that you didn't make a mistake. The truth is, Paris isn't a city you marry, it's a city you have an affair with; and the excitement, *malgré* the sodium lights, is everlasting.

January 31, 2008

LIFE @ THE WRITER'S ALMANAC

FOR nearly a year now, I've been waking up every morning with Garrison Keillor. Of all the men I've known, he's the best at getting me out of bed. He fills me with poetry, patiently educates me, and makes me smile. What more can a girl ask for?

The relationship began when I stumbled across *The Writer's Almanac* online (http://writersalmanac.org). I subscribed (it's free) and every morning it appears in my email, faithful and early. I sit down with a mug of hot coffee and read it before I do anything else. It begins with a poem, sometimes by contemporary poets I've never heard of, sometimes wandering around the centuries: Emily Dickinson, Gerard Manley Hopkins, Philip Larkin. Today, the poem was by Raymond Carver, called *In the Lobby of the Hotel del Mayo*. In 24 lines, Mr Carver tells how disaster intrudes into everyday life, and, even when the disaster has nothing to do with you, you never forget it. Right down my alley, you could say.

In the beginning I wasn't sure I wanted to read poetry online. I like slim volumes on ivory-white paper in Garamond font. But weeks can go by when I don't open a book. This way, the poem is like a gift that arrives each day, and it regularly leads me back to my shelves.

After the poem is a trio of anniversaries. Today is the birthday of the poet and novelist Richard Brautigan (1935). His novel *Trout Fishing in America* was on every cool bookshelf in the sixties. I never read it, but I remember the cover, a black-and-white photograph of Mr Brautigan standing with a woman. He committed suicide in the eighties, and I recall reading about his sad childhood and string of violent stepfathers. Mr Keillor gives a line from Brautigan that makes me wish I'd tackled his surreal and whimsical style: 'The sun was like a 50-cent piece that someone had poured kerosene on and then had lit a match, and said, "Here, hold this while I go get a newspaper", and put the coin in my hand, but never came back.'

Mr Keillor also notes that it's the birthday of the historian Barbara Tuchman (1912), whose book *The Guns of August* traces the events that lead to the First World War.

The third anniversary is not acknowledged in the British press. On this day in 1815, President James Madison approved an Act of Congress for the purchase of Thomas Jefferson's library of 6,487 volumes, at a cost of $23,950, a purchase made more urgent because, the year before, the British burnt down the US Capitol, destroying the

Library of Congress and its collection of 3,000 volumes.

I was brought up to believe that the war of 1812 was about as just as a war could be. That the British had been stopping and searching our ships, and taking off our seamen because they needed them to fight Napoleon. I'm always amazed that no one seems to know about the war of 1812. English friends are surprised when I tell them that the British burnt down the Capitol and the White House.

Still, my morning almanac on the internet, against the background of the *Today* programme, gives me other things to chew over. John Humphrys has just reported that we don't have enough trained troops to fight in Iraq and Afghanistan, so we're reducing the training time of our troops. My almanac begins to look like the fortune-teller's tea leaves: we're holding on to the burning 50-cent piece; and the miscalculations of these wars, financial and human, keep unfolding. Or, as Mrs Tuchman put it: 'War is the unfolding of miscalculations.'

February 7, 2008

AND THE WINNER IS...

I VOWED early on that when I won my Oscar I would wear a decent dress. Something elegant and cut on the bias. Think Katharine Hepburn. Or Audrey. I have never understood how actresses who look so stunning in the movies transform into hideous/kinky at the ceremony. Why don't they go to the costume designers who created their on-screen personas and say: '*Breakfast at Tiffany's*.' Even more mystifying: why are they always at a loss for words? Speaking is their job. Why can't they learn a few lines by heart just in case?

Perhaps this syndrome (call it Oscar Panic) appears so obvious to me because I've been practising my acceptance speech for five decades. In the early days I expressed my gratitude from the proscenium arch of the hayloft, addressing the mixed herd of Jersey and Guernsey cows below, a wide-eyed audience, attentive and appreciative. I fought back tears as I thanked my grandmother for giving me a set of matching Samsonite luggage and telling me to follow my dream.

As the years passed my dream changed. I got distracted by events and changed categories, moving from Best Performance by an Actress to Best Original Screenplay. During my Ingmar Bergman phase, I wrote a Southern Gothic script called *Mildew on the Magnolias*. During my Woody Allen period, I embarked on a prophetic science-fiction tale about all the good men (by this, I meant unmarried, straight and employed) mysteriously vanishing from Earth. I fell in love with the language of film – terms such as 'fade', 'dissolve' and 'cut'.

Life moves on. Opening scene: smoke billows from the sugar-beet factory. Camera scans landscape: fields of barley blowing in the wind. Close-up: the farmer's wife gazes at video shelves in the Ixworth Village Shop where country folk rent a movie for the weekend. Cut to: 10 years later and video shelves have been replaced by in-house bakery. Rural citizens did not suddenly prefer baguettes to *The Queen*, simply that free DVDs began tumbling out of the Sunday papers.

Every year as I listen to breathless expressions of gratitude, the linguistic fumbling that makes George W. Bush sound like a poet, I find myself gripping the sides of my stainless-steel podium. Leaning into the Fairy Liquid, gazing out on my audience of peacocks, chickens and sheep, I begin.

'Thank you all for your long-suffering patience. Despite the threats to your profession – foot-and-mouth, bluetongue, bird flu – you have been steadfast and I love you for it.

'Although you're too numerous to name, I have to thank all of you at The Agricultural Mortgage Corporation for your heart-felt belief in this farm. Without your faith, someone else might be standing at this podium tonight.

'And I want to thank all the taxpayers – you know who you are – who have given so unquestioningly to this moment, making possible the reservoir that will quench the thirst of the real stars of the future: carrots, onions, potatoes.

'I can't leave out Defra. We haven't always seen eye to eye, and I know I shouldn't mention it here tonight, but I'm afraid the badgers really have to go.

'Finally, I thank my husband, who gave me this starring role. Without him, where would I be? My heart is full.'

Applause. Dissolve.

March 6, 2008

LAMENTATION FOR THE DAY

EVERY year I try to begin Holy Week with the Book of Lamentations. It's a legacy from my father, a scholarly lay reader who believed it was spiritually lazy not to concentrate in the run-up to the most momentous event in the Christian calendar. I choose Lamentations because Ronald Blythe once wrote in the *Church Times* that this book from the Old Testament was his set text for Holy Week. He wrote that it thrilled him with the 'grandeur of its sadness'.

I've never experienced Blythe's thrill because I never reach the end. Although it's only five chapters long, I get worn down by the sorry state of Jerusalem and all its inhabitants. I also get distracted by my own difficult, everyday lamentations. Still, if the 'grandeur of sadness' is your thing, Holy Week 2008 was all you could ask for.

In a strange convergence of ecclesiastic calendar and modern history, Holy Week coincided with the fifth anniversary of the beginning of the war in Iraq. The days began with the *Today* programme recounting of those events, and ended each evening in front of the news with Jon Snow's reports on life in Iraq now. As the week progressed it felt more and more like a Mel Gibson re-enactment of Lamentations, with its historical setting of the fall of Jerusalem to the Babylonians, the destruction of the city, the abject conditions of those who were left behind.

Between the beginning and ending of these broadcast laments, lambs were born. Lambs arriving during Holy Week have a Biblical poignance. The Old Testament is full of shepherds looking for new pastures. The Gospel for the Sunday after Easter begins, 'Jesus said, I am the good shepherd.' All week long, our pastures were transformed into windswept tundras, with howling winds and bitter rain, hail and snow. Each morning, I tried to scoot the newborns and their mothers into the shed. Without a sheepdog, this is a job that requires picking up the lambs and encouraging their mothers to follow. There are no sheepdogs in the Bible either, an oversight that Jesus may have lamented during the parable of the lost sheep. Once inside the shed, I settle down, a lamb tucked inside my jacket, and my radio tuned into *Book of the Week*. The choice for Holy Week was Julian Barnes' *Nothing To Be Frightened Of*, a meditation on mortality and the fear of death. He begins: 'I don't believe in God, but I miss Him.'

By the time Easter Sunday arrived, the snow had descended like a veil over the countryside, a climatic version of the cloud in Lamentations, created so 'that our prayers should not pass through'. Modern theologians claim that Lamentations is not a breast-beating, self-pitying lament, but an account of a disaster that, without offering easy grace or cheap hope, tells us how to handle grief. It's a useful interpretation when there is much to grieve about. The cries of the bewildered ewes as we take away the lambs that didn't survive the freezing night. The milestone of '4,000 American soldiers dead' reached by Evensong on Easter Sunday. Tibetan monks dying for freedom. Houses repossessed.

I'm trying not to dwell on the 'grandeur of sadness', but to marvel at what has lived. Daffodils that survived the snow. Lambs that have begun their lamb games, and the bereaved ewe that has adopted a hungry triplet. The hope that some day even this war will end. And here's the Lamentation for the Day: you can believe in God and still miss Him.

April 3, 2008

LET EVENING COME

DIANA ATHILL begins her autumnal memoir *Somewhere Towards the End* looking out of her bedroom window at a pack of five pugs being walked in the park. The scene causes her a pang because she's always wanted a pug and now she's too old to get a puppy. She has a nice old dog, as old in dog years as she is – 89 when she was writing, now 90 – who is happy pottering along at her pace. A puppy requires house-training, lively walks and a game plan in case it outlives you.

I've been thinking about Miss Athill's book because, on Sunday, we collected Otis, our eight-week-old puppy, son of Bofus, our nine-year-old labrador. This wasn't a simple decision. Bofus (Southern for 'both of us') is a youthful old dog and fits into our lives perfectly. Like an only child who goes wherever you go, an only dog is portable. Once numbers increase, the whole show slows down.

On the plus side was the age-old theory that the puppy would rejuvenate the old dog, bringing companionship and fun to his twilight years. The pained look in Bofus's eyes as we presented him with his son suggests that notion is overworked. Although he's trying hard to be generous and self-effacing, Bofus has the anxious, puzzled look of one betrayed. In fact, he seems to have aged since Otis arrived, as though he's telling us that all he wants to do now is embrace his inner old dog.

I'm not insensitive to his dilemma. For one thing, I spend more and more time contemplating how humans embrace their inner old dog. Miss Athill's book nestles on an entire shelf on the subject, including an anthology that came out a couple of years ago called *Late Youth*, which celebrates the joys of being over 50; Katharine Whitehorn's memoir *Selective Memory*; Joan Bakewell's *The View From Here*, written when she reached 70; and Virginia Ironside's sparky and spiky novel *No! I Don't Want to Join a Book Club*. My copy of *Let Evening Come* by Mary C. Morrison, written in 1998 when the writer was 87, is well-worn and out of print.

Dwelling on age is compulsive. I study the presidential candidates and think there's a woman exactly my age who wants to run the world, more or less, and I'm daunted at running a farm, a family and house-training a puppy. I look at the candidate who's in his seventies and wonder if he's really up to the job. Until I look at his 95-year-old mother and think that she's livelier than her son.

Still, I never prepared for any of my journeys in life and,

with that little regret, I'm determined to prepare for this one. Miss Athill began by observing the women around her, including the writer Jean Rhys, who expected old age to make her miserable and it did. Miss Athill decided early on to avoid Miss Rhys's example. In *Late Youth*, Selina Hastings describes the shock of her age-conscious American friends as she snorted and heaved her way out of the car. 'Stop that! It makes you sound so old!' She now gets out of a car with the grace of a dancer.

If I'm honest, this puppy is rejuvenating me. I'm up at dawn and I'm walking 10 minutes every hour. The walks may not make me fitter, but they give me time to think. It may be too late for Diana Athill to get a puppy, but that's a small regret. All the big regrets she has wisely set aside and got on with what she likes doing best: reading, writing, friendships. She's my model for what to do later in life. And while I'm putting my plans for the twilight years in place, I'm emerging from the car looking like Ginger Rogers.

April 24, 2008

ALAS, WE HAVE CCTV

I KNOW it's *triste*, but, like E. F. Benson's Lucia, I think everything sounds better in French. For instance, 'L'Angleterre est une nation de boutiquiers' sounds like music to me, although it was Napoleon's idea of an insult. Saying that 'England is a nation of shopkeepers' really doesn't have the same ring to it. Which is not to say that I'm embarrassed to be a shopkeeper. It wasn't my dream as I set out in life but I like to think that I sell beautiful and useful goods that enhance life. I cringe when it's called a 'gift shop' because 'country store' has a purposeful and worthy sound that fits comfortably with the youthful idealist who once thought capitalism was the root of all evil.

During those high-minded years, I had a prized poster, sent to me by my friend Patty, who was on her junior year abroad in Paris. The year was 1968 and the poster, a clenched fist around the Eiffel Tower, read 'La propriété, c'est le vol'. In fact, I wasn't sure what it meant. I thought it said 'Propriety is robbery', a quirky slogan, but plausible. I soon learnt the correct translation – 'All property is theft', the rallying cry of the French anarchist Pierre-Joseph Proudhon. For years, the poster hung on my many kitchen walls; and, if only I'd kept it, would now fetch a hefty sum at Christie's South Kensington. The irony isn't lost on me.

But life and slogans move on. Now, if I saw 'All property is theft' posted, I'd scrawl beneath it, 'Let me rephrase that.' I'm spending the morning with John from Quantumatic, a company in Cambridge that sells CCTV cameras and alarm systems. He's explaining to me the differences between colour, black-and-white, quads, multiplexers and 4-8-16 cameras, as well as the significance of staticMini-Dome, SpeedDome, Standard-Resolution, High-Resolution. His mission is to help me create a 'secure retail environment'.

The array of digital technology in front of me is disheartening, but not as depressing as our need for it. Last Saturday, the most expensive item in the shop, a cashmere throw, was stolen. Sarah, the shop manager, had seen a young man in his early thirties looking at it, and noted that he didn't seem like he was in the market for cashmere. She alerted the other staff, but then there was a flurry of customers. Half an hour later, the throw (blue herringbone from Johnstons in Scotland, £350) and the man had disappeared.

This is the reality of being a shopkeeper today. Even if you're a country store in an idyllic setting, if you don't have a security system between 5% and 10% of your stock is lost to theft. As the economy worsens, shopkeepers are warned that shoplifting will increase. I try to decide (four cameras? eight?), wavering between despair and rage. Britain has the highest degree of surveillance in Europe. I think it's intrusive and plain creepy. But when cashmere throws (and books, Brio toys, Haws watering cans) disappear, a part of me wants to add a shotgun to my order. However, I calmly tell John that I want to find the system most likely to stop the crime before it starts, not shoot the thief in the act.

The shop staff are all in favour of the system, and I'm thinking of the wording for a hand-painted sign for my customers, who will be amazed and appalled at cameras in a store like mine. I know what Lucia would write: '"Surveillance", from the French *surveiller*, to watch over. As in: "Malheureusement, il faut surveiller".' But I'll settle for, 'Alas, we have CCTV.'

May 14, 2008

WORLD LAND TRUST

EVERY family has their share of secret shame. This is not the time for *True Confessions*, but when my husband's eyes get that distant look of sadness I know what he's thinking. Hedges. Miles of hedges that had defined the fields at Wyken since Domesday, and were the habitat of entire civilisations. Hedges that he bulldozed without mercy, in tune with the mantra of the times: big fields mean big yields/we've got to feed the world.

But life moves on. By the time we met, he was a Born Again farmer, a member of the 6ft Headlands and Beetle Bank faith. Wide grassstrips framed the fields, and hedges were being replanted. I reckoned I knew the worst about his past and all was forgiven.

Until last night. We were on our way to a very big event in Suffolk with Sir David Attenborough and the Ambassador from Paraguay, along with the heads of the World Land Trust (WLT) and Guyra Paraguay. We gathered in the rose garden at Thorpe Hall to witness the signing of an historic document, an agreement that will safeguard the future of the wildest place left on earth: the Dry Chaco in Paraguay.

This feels like the signing of a momentous peace treaty. Paraguay, a landlocked country in South America, has only recently emerged from years of dictatorships, and this document requires earthshaking optimism: the ambassador is signing away control of three national parks. For the next 10 years, some two-and-a-half million acres, an area the size of Yorkshire, will be run by Guyra Paraguay, an independent conservation organisation based in the country's capital.

Even more earthshaking, it will be funded by the small-but-beautiful WLT, which buys up land of great importance to the health of the planet and then turns that land over to the organisations in those countries that can look after it. Unlike the dot.com billionaires who sought to save the rainforests by buying them, the WLT buys the land on behalf of the cash-strapped conservation organisations in the countries. This secures the infrastructure needed to protect the land from poachers, loggers and invaders who ruthlessly clear the land for soya and cattle farming. The WLT, guided by its remarkable co-founder John Burton, has always put sustainability first. John has no idea where he'll get the £10 million for this historic salvation of the Dry Chaco, but the miracle is getting the agreement. Compared with that, the money is easy.

Somewhere between the town of Eye and the barn where

we watch the 50-year-old film by Sir David Attenborough called *Zoo Quest* in Paraguay, my husband confesses new shame: in his twenties, he spent a year in Paraguay working for Liebig's. While he was there, the meat company bought up 80,000 acres of rainforest and cleared it for grazing. It was called Progress, twin sister to Prosperity.

All evening my husband looks uneasy. So does Sir David Attenborough, who is watching a film of a younger version of himself. On the screen, bottom in the air, he is digging with his bare hands the hole that's home to a family of baby armadillos – quadruplets. He gives each of the babies a little kiss on the nose before stuffing them in cotton sacks and placing them on the oxwagon, the first stage of their long journey to the London Zoo. Their bereaved mother is never mentioned.

Many are the sins committed through ignorance. Lucky is the man who lives long enough to redeem himself. Sir David wouldn't kidnap baby armadillos now, and truly no one has done more than this saintly man to inform and alert the world to the precious and vulnerable wilderness left on our planet.

My husband's penitence has been more modest. As he watches the men signing, he looks tearful. I feel more hedges are on the way, along with some serious fundraising for the Dry Chaco.

June 25, 2008

THE FIRE THIS TIME

THE smell of smoke is coming through the window as I write. It is not the smell of autumn, of leaves burning. It is the smell of 30 bales of straw, burning all through the night. Burning through the shifts of three fire crews from the next-door village of Ixworth. It is the smell of anger and futility. It is the smell of arson on a farm that is recorded in the pages of Domesday. It is the smell of the times in which we live.

Adrian Delaney, a professional fireman with the Ministry of Defence, is part of the second crew. He tells me we are lucky. The wind could easily have carried the fire to the surrounding wheat fields, and we would have lost this year's crops. The fire could have crossed the road and swallowed three cottages with it. The fire could have entered the ancient woodlands separated by a field of wheat. As he describes our good fortune, I stare at the straw mountain. It looks black and subdued, but as the firemen drag their rakes across the surface blazes leap up. Conversation fades as we watch, mesmerised by the tenacity of the flaming monster and all the ways in which this deliberate act of stupidity could have turned into a disaster.

I tell Adrian all I know. Steve, one of our tractor drivers, arrived in the farmyard at 9.30pm with the plough. He locked up and went home. Nothing was amiss. At 9.45pm, the fire station in Ixworth was called and a fire reported. The caller's telephone number was 'unavailable'. The fire engine arrived at 10pm and saw a moped speed off. No one who lives in the cottages across the road was home. We got a call at 10.15pm to tell us about the fire, and ran down the drive. Adrian looks into the distance as he tells me that investigations of fires are time-consuming and rarely turn up anything. Courses in forensic psychology don't tend to dwell on arsonists very long because too much of the evidence is destroyed in the crime.

Lurking in my heart is the feeling that the bales should never have been in that field – the overflow car park for the farmer's market – and certainly not next to the road. Last week, there was a bale fire on the A143 on a neighbouring farm. As soon as harvest begins, pyromaniacal paranoia sets in. That's why you see bale mountains stacked high in the middle of fields, straw Lego creations that can only be reached by tractors and combines. A man with a blowtorch would think twice about trying to cover that distance and get away without being seen.

My husband and I react differently to fire. I carry

the burden of memory. My grandparents watched their wooden house in the Mississippi Delta burn to the ground and spent the rest of their lives remembering things they had lost. On my grandmother's desk were three pieces of modern art: pieces of silver that her mother had brought from Sweden, melted into abstract shapes that might have been from the studio of Salvador Dali. My legacy is one of hysteria and fear of fire.

My husband possesses a practical spirit. 'We won't put bales in vulnerable places again.' He reminds me of hen-house civilisation. You only need a couple of hens to go berserk every time you enter the hen house to incite the whole flock to craziness. Remove the jumpy hens that trigger mass panic and the other hens return to their easy-going, gentle selves.

With the hen-house rules in mind, I'm trying to be calm about the fire. I'm not heading off in my usual direction, bucking and snorting about the state of the country, but deep down I feel as jumpy as a nervous hen. The fire is dying down, but my eyes are still burning.

August 20, 2008

IN THE LAND OF BOFUS

FOR some time now we've been meaning to get a new map made of Wyken. We have faded maps that were drawn by meticulous mapmakers in the 17th and 18th centuries, maps that show fields and woodlands on a human scale, but our only modern maps of the estate look like satellite-navigation projects required by Defra.

The reason for the delay is a conflict of desire. I want a map that has the poetry of our ancient maps, a map that looks like the wrapping paper Matthew Rice created in the Eighties, with watercolour fields dotted with sheep and cows, and trees that look like bunches of broccoli. A map you might call Pastoral Romantic. My husband wants a map that accurately records fields and the exact legal boundaries of our land deeds. While we've hemmed and hawed, we've planted thousands of trees, an ambitious attempt to block out the lights and noise from the A143 two miles away. We've laid miles of hedges, remorse for those ripped out 30 years ago. Best of all, we've created two lakes: Lake Bofus and Big Bofus.

Nobody gets it at first. And then I explain that 'Bofus' is southern for 'both of us', that the two farm workers on my grandmother's dairy farm never did anything single-handed. Whatever the job, Dude would say, 'Bofus can do it', and off he'd go with Plez to grab a bale of hay, move the cows to another field, kill the snake curled up in the chicken house. Bofus became part of our secret language as children, and, in a fit of nostalgia, the name of a much-loved friend and companion, a fox-red Labrador.

If our new map of Wyken survives as long as the maps hanging in the back hall, the name Bofus might stick out. After Bofus the dog, we just went wild. First, there was two-acre Lake Bofus (now known as Baby Bofus); then, inspired by that lake, we created Big Bofus, a four-acre lake. Out of the earth excavated for Big Bofus, we created a steep hill we christened Mount Bofus. Overlooking the wetland loved by dragonflies is Swamp Bofus. The whole area, a vast wildflower meadow, is now called Yellow Dog National Park, a name that lacks the Englishness of a Suffolk estate that is older than America.

My favourite routine over the past few years has been the walk up to Big Bofus with the lake's canine namesake at my side. I take a Thermos of coffee, a book and a cushion, and Bofus and I get into the Old Town canoe and glide around the lake like a Buick on a Sunday afternoon drive. We stop in the middle, and, while I read, Bofus keeps an eye out for fish. He never looks bored. We could be a cover for the L. L. Bean catalogue.

But lakes live longer than dogs. On Saturday, we took Bofus to the vet in Diss because the ear infection we'd been treating all summer was getting worse. The vet suspected a tumour and told us to prepare for the worst. In fact, we'd been preparing for the worst all summer long.

The vet gave us options. An MRI scan at £1,500. A delicate operation in Cambridge that would require the skill of a veterinary neurologist: £3,000. A prolonged convalescence with no guarantee that the tumour would not come back. We hope we made our decision based on what was best for a nine-year-old dog. We wanted his last memories in life to be swimming out to the canoe and carrying the paddle back to shore in his mouth.

When we finally get around to commissioning our map, I want a fox-red dog sitting upright in a canoe in the middle of Lake Bofus. It may mystify future rural historians, but Bofus was a dog worthy of his place in the history of the Suffolk landscape. Meanwhile, we console ourselves with the wisdom of S. J. Perelman: 'Outside of a dog, a book is a man's best friend,' he wrote. 'Inside of a dog, it's too dark to read.'

September 3, 2008

THE WHISTLEJACKET REDEMPTION

WHEN the story of these dark and troubled days comes to be written, a historian might well begin with the two-day sale of dead butterflies and pickled animals held at Sotheby's in September. The carnage made a record £95.7 million for artist Damien Hirst. A cabinet of fish skeletons and stuffed fish (£2.95 million) had the title *Here Today, Gone Tomorrow*, words that have a resonance no historian worth his First at Balliol could ignore.

If the historian is tempted to begin his account earlier, he could consider 2004, when the hedge-fund broker Steve Cohen paid £12 million for a third of a ton of shark that was already showing signs of decay (Cohen paid another $100,000 to restore his dead fish). Or the moment last year when the famous diamond-encrusted skull was revealed to a worshipful art world. But I would advise the historian to focus on Hirst's *The Golden Calf*, with a gold disc on its head and hoofs made of real gold.

Ah, the god of gold. On the day that Wall Street recorded

its greatest losses ever, the British Museum unveiled a 110lb solid-gold statue of the model Kate Moss. The museum described Marc Quinn's sculpture as the 'Aphrodite of our times'. As citizens throughout the land were trembling in fear for their jobs, pensions and savings, the National Portrait Gallery launched a public appeal to raise £200,000 for another Quinn sculpture: a self-portrait head made of the artist's own frozen blood. In fact, the head costs £350,000, but the Art Fund has offered a £100,000 grant and the National Portrait Gallery has found £50,000 from its own resources. On the day the country of Iceland went bankrupt, Charles Saatchi opened his new gallery in the 205-year-old Duke of York's grand military headquarters. The exhibition features art from China, including a giant turd on the floor packed with toy soldiers.

Never has art so painfully imitated life: art-world greed reflected in the mirror of financial world greed, the con artists in the City and on Wall Street setting the stage for the con artists of the art world. I'm as ashamed of the British Museum, the National Portrait Gallery and the Art Fund (of which I am a life member) for their complicity in the fatuous and greed-crazed art world as I am of the leaders of the banking world who have destroyed their institutions and devastated the lives of so many men and women.

Decadence on this scale leaves a bitter taste. It also has terrible side effects. Money spent on dismal, fraudulent and dead art means that the rare and genuine gets neglected.

In the middle of last week's turmoil, I saw an exhibition in Leeds Art Gallery. Entitled 'Whistlejacket and Scrub: Large as Life', it features the horse paintings of Stubbs. It isn't vast like the exhibition at the Tate in 1985, but it unites for the first time in 250 years two great paintings: *Whistlejacket*, one of Britain's most loved works, saved for the nation by the Heritage Lottery Fund in 1997, and *Scrub*, *Whistlejacket*'s brother, and the only one of Stubbs' life-size portraits of horses still owned privately.

This exhibition, the brainchild of Sir Nicholas Brooksbank, very nearly didn't happen. The sponsor, a property developer in Leeds, began feeling the tremors of the financial earthquake before the ink of the catalogue was dry. But having persuaded the National Gallery to loan *Whistlejacket*, and Lord Halifax his newly restored *Scrub*, Sir Nicholas was determined that the historic reunion of the two horses would go on.

These are not animals that have been embalmed and preserved by someone who does not understand nature. Stubbs' majestic horses are inspirational animals preserved by genius. They will probably never be seen together again, but they fulfil what I yearn for in art: beautiful, and very difficult to execute. This is art with redemptive spirit. Go and gaze at *Whistlejacket* and *Scrub* and wonder how we got so lost.

October 15, 2008

MANNERS MAKETH MARRIAGE

THE choir sings the *Introit* in the ante-chapel. It is *Locus iste* by Bruckner, but I know this only because it's written on the order of service for this choral evensong. The music does what Jesus exhorts his disciples to do: to be in the world, but not of it. Winchester College Chapel is as old as the school itself and, despite its diminutive size – originally designed to seat a scholarly congregation of just over 100 – its fan-vaulted ceiling lifts the spirit today just as it has been doing for more than 600 years.

Friends and family have made the journey to Hampshire to celebrate Martin and Petronella's 40th wedding anniversary, and the celebration begins with Evensong. The world outside the chapel is a shaky place: economies around the world are crumbling, a momentous presidential race is reaching its final days, and papers are in riotous mood with a feud between shadow chancellors and old friends. Meanwhile, inside this chapel, we have gathered to celebrate the bonds that hold us together in difficult times: family, friendship, faith and married love.

Leaving the world behind, being in it but not of it, isn't easy. I'm part of the Oxford circle. My husband was at Magdalen with Martin, and we are here with other friends from the Oxford years: Nick and Susanna, whose own 40th anniversary was celebrated at Christ Church last summer, against a backdrop of miracles in Nick's battles with cancer; Simon, whose wife, Annabel, died three years ago from one of those cancers that moves quietly and quickly; John and Ginny, looking youthful and happy, her cancer in remission. Each warm embrace is followed by a searching look – how are you? how are you *really*?

As the choir sings the *Magnificat*, I think about these friendships that are older than the marriage we are here to celebrate. I think also about the importance of friendships in married lives, the shared histories, the tapestry of godchildren, the archives of memory. A significant anniversary is not only a celebration of love and longevity; it's a recognition of the friendships that bolster a marriage, providing the outside support, distraction and comfort that strengthens all marriages.

My eyes focus on the Wykehamist motto printed on the front of the service sheet: 'Manners Makyth Man.' Manners now seems an antique word, but it was the moral code drilled into us by Southern grandmothers: 'Manners are more important than brains.'

Wykehamists are famous for their good brains, but

for a good marriage manners are vital. They are a form of wisdom: you do not say the hurtful words; you commit to the politics of shutting up. Manners are the kindness that is at the heart of married love.

The familiar beauty of the *Nunc dimittis* lifts me out of my wandering. The virtue of music at Evensong is that of spiritual awareness, which used to be called 'recollection'. I remember why I'm here: I married into this tapestry of friendships. Even now, halfway towards a Ruby anniversary, I can't believe my good luck.

I wish I could produce a little nugget of truth about married love and friendships, but instead I'll give you something cheerful. Go to Google and type in 'The Oxford Clerks', and you'll find a six-man close-harmony *a cappella* group, all choral scholars at New College and Magdalen. Click on 'Music' and listen to *A Nightingale Sang in Berkeley Square*. Here's the truth: close harmony in friendship, marriage and song is worth celebrating.

November 5, 2008

TESTAMENT OF HOPE

I BEGAN supporting 'Obama for President' back in the summer of 1964 when he was three years old. I'm not sure of the exact day, but it might have been in the early hours just before dawn when I sat with my father in our living room, looking out on the front yard. He had a shotgun in his lap and a glass of Jim Beam bourbon and water at his side. He was determined that the 'sons of bitches' who had burned a cross the night before wouldn't do it again. He didn't plan to shoot them, just to 'scare the hell out of the damned cowards'.

The Klan in our small Mississippi town had been fairly dormant for a decade or so, but the summer of '64 triggered renewed fury in the white-sheeted brethren. They saw a very real threat to their way of life: a movement aided by an influx of northern white college students whose mission was to register black citizens to vote. The thought of a ballot box filled with black votes led to the burning and bombing of black churches and homes, five churches in my home town alone. My father, a lay-reader in the Episcopal church, tried to bring black and white clergymen together to form a coalition calling for peace. It was a modest step, but it led to burning crosses, bomb threats and social isolation. We ended up leaving the town, and, finally, the state where my grandfather had been a member of the state legislature and a county prosecuting attorney for 50 years.

Like many acts of violence, the Klan's attempts to silence my family backfired. My parents changed almost overnight from gentle Southern liberals into dedicated foot soldiers in the Civil Rights movement, my mother marching in Selma, my father organising legal protection for blacks registering to vote in Albany and Americus, Georgia. Their home in Maryland became a refuge for weary Civil Rights workers, black and white, in need of a few days' warmth and shelter. When Lyndon Johnson signed into law the Voting Rights Act in 1965, they both wept. My father believed it was the most important piece of legislation since the Constitution, that it would make the Bill of Rights a reality.

If I ever wondered if Barack Obama was presidential, any doubts ended last March, when he gave his speech entitled 'A More Perfect Union'. The Lincoln scholar Garry Wills later made comparisons between Mr Obama's speech and a speech given by Lincoln in 1860. Two young men from Illinois, both lawyers, both seeking his party's nomination against a New York senator of great repute, both known for opposing an initially popular war: Lincoln against President Polk's Mexican war; Mr Obama against President Bush's Iraq war. And both men were accused of associations with extremists: Lincoln of supporting Abolitionists who had burned the Constitution; Mr Obama of supporting an inflammatory preacher who had damned the U.S.

As remarkable as these coincidences, however, was the vision of America professed in the two speeches. With restrained optimism and solemn pragmatism, Lincoln and Mr Obama both spoke of a civilisation that can improve itself. Mr Obama's belief throughout the long campaign has been that America can be better.

I know there are dark days ahead. Mr Obama inherits a terrible legacy. But I'm celebrating the success of a man who can articulate feelings and ideas. President-Elect Obama may not have the profound eloquence of Lincoln, but, after a parched eight years, he sounds like a prince of language. And I'm glad to have lived long enough to see that the Promised Land – the land promised by the Constitution – is in view. The day after the election, I swear I could hear my father's soft voice repeating his favourite words from the abolitionist Theodore Parker, often quoted by Martin Luther King: 'The arc of the moral universe is long, but it bends towards justice.'

November 12, 2008

HOME ON THE RANGE

THE day after my grandfather's funeral, my grandmother sold the dairy. Her granddaughters were shocked at her heartless farewell to the pedigreed herd of Jerseys that she'd spent 30 years building up. We bade tearful goodbyes to our tender and loveable companions.

'Cows are not tender and loveable,' my grandmother snapped. 'They are anxious, neurotic and moody.' And so was she after years of getting up in the dark for milking and rushing home every evening in time to milk again while our grandfather sat on the porch reading Gibbon and Darwin and saying how a field of cows made him feel at peace with the world.

To our mind, when the cows went, the farm died. The dairy still had the smell of sour milk and hay; and we would spend hours in blank lamentation, sitting in the cool, empty space. Over time, the milking parlour began to fill up with broken pieces of farm machinery, plants that needed to be inside in winter, and piles of croker sacks whose grassy smell reminded us of the cows.

Then my Uncle Sidney decided to bring the farm back to life. He decided to buy cattle. Meat cattle. Aberdeen Angus. Sleek, glossy and black. The cattle would be the answer to everyone's prayers: scenic fields, minimal agricultural taxes on the land and nothing to do but watch the young steers grow to be the size of Pontiacs in the shadow of their mothers.

Faithless as we were, we soon transferred our affections to these new creatures. Our grandmother was right: the Angus cattle were as calm as house cats. They came to us when we called them, loved having their foreheads rubbed, and had a soulful look that made us think of God. Somehow the truck that came in the spring to take away the boys always came when we were at school, and within a very short time we had new calves to love. There was only one small problem: like almost every farmer who went into beef cattle, my uncle nearly went bankrupt.

And so it came to pass that when I married a farmer I came with a bovine yearning. Not the perpetually menstrual dairy cows – I've watched my friend and neighbour Jane Capon work herself to the bone with her organic herd of Jerseys. In any case, I long ago converted the old dairy into a country store and the bullpen into a café for the farmer's market. Nope. I wanted cattle. More specifically, I wanted Suffolk cattle: those deep-chestnut, conker-red cattle called Red Polls ('polled' cattle means 'without horns'.) Fellow barley barons of East Anglia sniffed at the idea. 'Cattle are the crop of City bankers who want to decorate their country acres, non-farmers who want ambiance.' My husband was reluctant. 'Who's going to look after them?' He also dreaded my days of grief when the boys would go off and reappear on the restaurant menu.

But, last week, at the gathering at The Rose and Crown after Reg Frost's funeral, I heard about a small herd for sale in Cockfield. The farmers were retiring and moving to Scotland.

This morning, my small herd arrived: Norah, aged 17, with her two-month-old calf at her side; Ruby with her four-month-old calf; and three more girls who have calved once. Red Polls are maternal, light-footed and beautiful. Mine come from a hand-reared herd, and are affectionate and sociable.

My husband is content because they will graze his precious wildflower meadows and fulfil the requirements for the Higher Level Stewardship Scheme. I am happy because the field looks like a painting by Constable, the low mooing sound is as spiritual as a Gregorian chant, and the smell is more evocative than anything dreamt of by Proust. I've kept vague about the economics of my beautiful new family, and I look the other way when folks murmur 'hamburger'. Right now, I'm enjoying the quiet exultation of cows at Wyken. Life is good when the cows come home.

November 19, 2008

VI

Late Harvest

A WINTER'S TALE

ALL week long it felt as if a state of grace had descended on the countryside. Frost turned the hedgerows into diamond mines that glistened in the dull daylight. The peacocks huddled together for warmth, their gaudy feather tapestry the only thing visible under the duvet of fog. For the pheasants, it was a welcome reprieve: the guns surrendered and came in early, but not before testing the ice that covered the reservoir, ice as thick as the London *Yellow Pages*, ice solid enough for skaters. Who can be sure? Ice is as exotic in this part of Suffolk as polar bears.

Despite the shivering, the cold is welcome. In the horticultural world, they call it *vernalisation*, a period of cold required by a plant to initiate flowering. People need it, too. These seasonless years deprive us of ceremony and understanding, and there is no health in it. One wintry ceremony that has been on hold for too long: blueberry pancakes and streaky bacon. A jug of maple syrup presides over the kitchen, its simple label a work of art: Pure

Maine Maple Syrup, Made by Everett Moulton, South Parsonsfield, Maine. In fact, the contents aren't made by Everett, who gave up sugaring when he was 95. This is maple syrup from L. L. Bean, decanted into one of Everett's old jugs by my friend Susan, one-time resident of Parsonsfield. Every year she arrives at Wyken with a new harvest of maple syrup and vintage Everett stories. It's right that we should begin this cold-as-Maine day with a ceremony of pancakes, because last night Susan called to tell us that Everett had died.

Everett's expression of the verb to die was 'get through', as in 'Everett Moulton got through on Friday'. He was born in 1909, and in September would have been 100. When he married Minnie in 1927, they moved into the house, a classic New England centre chimney cape, next door to his family's farm on Moulton Hill. His farm of 230 acres marched beside his family's place, another 150 acres including about 50 acres of ancient stone-walled fields, which he mowed with a tractor he had made from an old Ford truck, pulling the trailer he had constructed out of hefty timbers.

The hay was feed for his cattle, a herd he restricted to 14. He'd slaughter one a year for the house, but the rest was his capital. He kept the herd until he was 95. When he finally sold it, he kept one old cow for companionship. His animals informed his view of life. He liked to describe the birth of a calf. 'When it first comes out, it is lifeless. After a little nudge and a few licks, it suddenly comes to life. And that's all that separates life and death: a few licks.'

The farmer-philosopher was caretaker of the land and caretaker of the local cemetery. Solemn and practical, he dug all the graves by hand long past the arrival of the mechanical digger, faithful to his belief in the superiority of the handmade grave over the machine hole. He'd begin by cutting and peeling off a neat rectangle of sod with the skill of a tailor cutting priceless cloth, carefully lifting it to one side. After the funeral, he would fill in the hole and replace the grassy blanket with such precision that you couldn't tell that the earth had been disturbed.

With his respect for the earth and a barn filled with the machinery of another age – scythes, pitchforks – Everett's life was like a poem by Walt Whitman, a song by Aaron Copland, an essay by Wendell Berry. A farmer whose knowledge of culture and agriculture, of man, animals, the weather and the land, follows him into the grave he dug for himself. I'd like to think that he will be taken there in the 1936 pick-up that sits in his barn, the truck he drove for 70 years until, reluctantly, he gave up driving aged 97. Even now, I can hear him speculating on life after death. 'They must find good work up there,' he'd say with a straight face, 'because they don't come back to Parsonsfield.'

January 21, 2009

LETTER FROM WASHINGTON

WE set out in dawn's early light, wrapped in so many layers that our knees and elbows can't bend. Our starting point is Washington's National Cathedral, its Gothic twin towers a faithful compass for citizens of the nation's capital. Today it's also a compass for our history: it was in this cathedral that Martin Luther King Jr gave his last Sunday sermon just days before going to Memphis and the assassin's bullet.

Our group of pilgrims, a cousinage of two generations, is evenly divided, the under-21 brigade a fast-moving air-traffic control, monitoring history on their BlackBerries. 'The Stanford group found a cab and are already on the Mall,' Cooper tells us. 'The line outside Union Station is now six blocks long,' reports Gabriel, who, at 18, was the youngest field organiser in the campaign, spending his gap year working 12-hour days in Montgomery County, Pennsylvania. I hear my son relay events to friends in Edinburgh. The old folks' thoughts are harder to share. We're three white Southerners who grew up in a landscape where 'White' and 'Colored' divided water fountains and waiting rooms, where the myth of 'Separate but Equal' deluded our schools, and the black people we knew could not vote. We left that world behind long ago, but its legacy, like knuckle tattoos of 'Love' and 'Hate', never fades completely.

Two miles on, numbed by the Siberian temperatures, I'm guiltily wondering if this Long Walk is such a good idea. Suddenly, an empty cab and an SUV appear and offer to take us 'as close as we can get'. It's four miles of heated deliverance, and the magnitude of the miracle is revealed when we reach the Mall and head towards our destination: Blue Gate. We will walk, wait, stand and inch forward for four-and-a-half hours, longer than I've ever waited for anything. And we're the lucky ones, clutching precious tickets to the crescent below the inaugural platform. All 230,000 of us. The other two million stretch out for two miles beyond.

As we wait, we feel something. It's like the Sam Cooke song that goes, 'There's something's happening here', and the happening is a big-hearted happiness. 'This is incredible. It feels like a scene from the Bible,' says a man behind me. 'Or a movie,' says his daughter. We sing, chant 'O-ba-ma' and 'Yes we can', talk to strangers and say reluctant farewells when the flow of the crowd heaves us apart. No one complains in this jubilant new world of endless patience.

When we enter the Promised Land, it's almost noon. We crane our necks to see a giant screen. Two black women behind me identify all the dignitaries as they appear. When Laura Bush arrives, the crowd falls silent. When Michelle

309

Obama appears, we go wild. When George Bush emerges, 'boos' begin to swell, but the women behind me give orders to the crowd. 'Shush!' they say. 'Show some respect!' The crowd obeys. Finally, the new President arrives, young and handsome in his overcoat. Then the screen shows us what he sees: a crowd that stretches into infinity, like a vast field of barley blowing in the wind.

The simple oath is only 35 words long. The Inaugural Address is a sombre 18 minutes in which President Obama moves from 'Hope' to the bleaker reality of 'Hope against hope'. There's no single phrase that we'll always remember, but this is a crowd that knows that 'nothing to fear but fear itself' is palpably untrue; there is much, much else to fear.

What gives us hope is the sense that a new day has come. We feel it when the new President says 'so help me God', and again when we look up in the sky at the helicopter taking the former President to the airport. A stunned silence, followed by a roar as a million hands wave farewell. Then, a lone voice in the crowd, a baritone as deep as Paul Robeson's, begins to sing:

My country 'tis of thee, Sweet land of liberty, Of thee I sing.

Slowly the crowd joins in, singing the words they know by heart:

Land where my fathers died, Land of the pilgrims' pride,
From ev'ry mountainside let freedom ring!

February 4, 2009

TRY TO REMEMBER

I CAN never remember if *Desert Island Discs* is broadcast on Sunday and repeated on Friday, or the other way round. I've missed many rendezvous with interesting people because of this chronic memory lapse, and you can't go to 'Listen Again' because of copyright issues with the music*. Still, thanks to a Post-it note last Friday, I managed to hear David Suchet.

It was fascinating to learn that the actor's father, a surgeon, was disappointed with his middle son's lack of academic purpose. That, age eight, he was sent with his older brother John to a boarding school on the Kent coast, where they were forced to swim in the sea year round. The image of the two little boys holding hands and walking into the freezing water singing *You'll Never Walk Alone* was heartbreaking. But things got better. It was love at first sight when he met the actress Sheila Ferris in 1972 at the Belgrade Theatre in Coventry; on their first date, sitting on

---

* Now you can listen to All Desert Island Discs.

a bench at 3am, he burst into 'When I fall in love, it will be forever'. And he did. They are still married and in love.

It's impossible to separate David Suchet from Hercule Poirot, especially now when, thanks to the digital ITV3 channel, I watch Agatha Christie's fastidious Belgian detective over and over. My memory is so rickety that I can never recall whodunnit, which may explain why I'm so fond of *Desert Island Discs*.

Despite claims that the lemony scent of *madeleines* is the greatest trigger of memory, I believe it is music that opens the rusty latches of the past. All week long, I've been singing *When I Fall in Love* to my cows, a mournful maternity whose calves are being weaned two fields away. I hope my singing comforts them. It soothes me because I know all the words and I can also remember playing it over and over again, aged 16, when I first fell in love. I'm convinced that music is the live wire in the brain that functions longest, leaving us hymns and carols long after the names of lovers and rivers have vanished.

All the same, watching repeats of *Poirot* with the same wonderment of the first viewing led me to follow up David Suchet with Terry Pratchett's remarkable account on BBC2 of his first year with Alzheimer's, which, in the zeitgeist of dementia, coincided with the interview in the *Daily Telegraph* with John Suchet, the protective older brother, who only days before had been wading into the sea as a little boy. Now he was revealing the heartache of watching his beloved wife, Bonnie, three years into her descent into Alzheimer's. With trembling heart, I began to read a book I bought last summer by Sue Halpern called *Can't Remember What I Forgot.*

First, the bad news. By 2025, dementia is expected to strike 34 million people globally. Half of all people who reach age 85 will exhibit some symptoms of the disease. The good news? The other half won't. Watching Mr Pratchett's search for strategies and delays was encouraging, because even with Alzheimer's his is a formidable brain. Miss Halpern's assurance is for the 'worried well' living in the fog of pre-dementia. She explains that middle-age memory loss is perfectly normal; that as we get older we all suffer from ADHD, attention-deficit *hypo*activity – not *hyper*activity. Our attention flickers, but it's not that we forget. We simply don't concentrate as well as we used to.

Neuroscientists are developing drugs (called guanfacine) that revitalise concentration and memory in rats. Meanwhile, the scientists are firm on this. Exercise. Walk two miles a day. Briskly. Mice who take to the treadmill produce nice new neurons. Sedentary mice do not. And eat blueberries. They fight the atoms that damage brain tissue. I would add to this recipe for Memory: stick with *Poirot* and Nat King Cole. In a restless world like this is, love is ended before it's begun.

February 25, 2009

313

THE MEANING OF BROWN EGGS

'NEVER compound ignorance with inaudibility,' my grandmother advised whenever I tried to mumble my way through something I didn't understand. It's advice that I've followed, modifying it only in moments of total ignorance, when I try to practise silence.

These have been rich times for mumbling softly because, frankly, I don't know what's going on. For a start, I don't understand the language. Hedge funds. Derivatives. Credit swaps. Leveraged buyouts. Subprime. Even when I have a vague idea of the meaning, I don't know how it works. I can't see how printing money (quantitative easing) won't cause inflation. More confusing: if the kernel of the credit crisis was the billions of dollars of mortgages handed out to subprime (unsuitable) borrowers in America, loans that went sour as borrowers defaulted, how can the solution now be to use taxpayer money to buy the subprime 'toxic assets'?

I'm not proud of my financial ignorance. I believe

that if you don't understand how money (complicated and messy) works, you won't really understand how life (complicated and messy) works. The writer J. B. Priestley once wrote about a discovery that moved him into 'the vast invisible realm where our lives are shaped'. I've always thought that money was the 'invisible realm', and one day I made a great discovery about how my life was shaped. I had a £1,000 debt on my Visa card and I discovered that if I only paid off the minimum each month it would take 18 years to clear it.

The revelation that moved Priestley into his invisible realm was more down to earth. It was his discovery that Americans prefer white eggs. In an article entitled *The Meaning of Brown Eggs*, he wrote that Americans 'despise brown eggs because they seem closer to nature'. White eggs are better, 'especially if they are to be given to precious children, because their very whiteness suggests hygiene and purity'. However, his fellow countrymen 'prefer the brown egg because it belongs to the enduring dream of the English, who always hope sooner or later to move into the country'. The rich brown egg is the very symbol of nature, of English country living.

Although my ignorance about money and finance may be impenetrable, my friend and neighbour, Francine Raymond, known in these parts as 'the chicken woman', has penetrated my egg ignorance. All eggs, she told me – brown, white, taupe or duck-egg blue – are exactly the same under the skin. Pigmentation of the shell has nothing to do with the taste or nutritional merit of the egg. For flavour, you must go to the heart of the egg: the yolk. My Dark Brahma hens lay eggs of deep saffron yellow because they have a rich diet of greenery, including primroses, hellebores and tulips. I sigh in wonder as my fork lances the poached egg; I say a silent prayer of gratitude as sourdough soldiers pierce the soft-boiled gift.

But concluding deep differences about cultures – American *vs.* English – based on egg colour preference is dubious scholarship. The preference for white eggs stems from the breed. The Leghorn, the greatest egg-laying machine known to man, lays white eggs. My Brahmas, as feckless as southern belles, produce rich-brown eggs.

And what does this have to do with the impenetrable financial mess we are in? I reckon any form of enlightenment in these dark times is welcome. My grandmother had something to say about eggs and bacon as well. 'Respect your breakfast,' she announced each morning. 'A day's work for the chicken. A lifetime commitment for the pig.'

April 1, 2009

BETWEEN GRIEF AND HOPE

THE beginning of Holy Week began for me one day last summer when I made my way to Borough High Street in search of St George the Martyr Church. I was looking for the workshop behind the church where the artist Craigie Aitchison makes his screenprints. I love his work, but all I've ever owned is a mouse mat from the Royal Academy shop. In August, I decided to go further. The picture I had in mind was the postcard-sized *Lamb in a Green Field*.

Sister Wendy believes that some artists seem to use images that speak of the mystery of God. She thinks that Mr Aitchison is one of those artists. Under her influence, I saw my Aitchison lamb as a kind of Agnus Dei, but when I found the Advanced Graphics workshop and studied the picture I did not see a lamb that was the symbol of Jesus Christ in his role of the perfect sacrificial offering that atones for the sins of humanity. I saw a white lamb in a green field against a blue sky.

I don't think the artist would be troubled by my failure

to see the religious imagery. Mr Aitchison is one of the few contemporary artists to paint convincing Christian pictures, but he leaves ecclesiastical interpretation to others. In any case, my decision not to buy the lamb wasn't theological. I simply saw another picture by the artist. One of Christ on the cross.

Crucifixion paintings are an important theme in Mr Aitchison's work. The cross is always in a landscape, isolated and alone. Often, the cross is in front of Holy Isle by the slope on Arran where the ashes of the artist's parents are scattered. Occasionally, there is a lamb nearby, but in the artist's *Crucifixion* that hangs in King's College Chapel there is only the solitary figure of Christ.

The picture I chose shows Christ on the cross against a dark sky, with a dog (his Bedlington Terrier) at the foot, gazing upwards, one paw lifted. Perched on one arm of the cross are two birds. Above the head of Christ is a white dove. It was an impetuous purchase. I set out to buy a picture the size of a dollar bill, and I bought a picture the size of a duvet. The only wall large enough for it was on the stairs, where a 17th-century tapestry hangs. The picture now hangs over the tapestry.

But size was a minor problem compared with the subject. Unless it's 300 years old and you inherited it, a picture of Christ on the cross hanging in your house makes folks nervous. Reactions to the Aitchison *Crucifixion* are either, 'Nice, but I wouldn't want to live with it', or sheer

Dawkinsian disbelief that I could display such lack of taste and intelligence, responses that make me babble about the artist's secular credentials: born in Scotland, son of a Law Lord who became Lord Provost of Edinburgh, studied at the Slade, Royal Academician who resigned over the Saatchi 'Sensation' show. I gently suggest that the painting captures human suffering, the grey dog with his uplifted foot speaks of grief, the white dove symbolises hope. I sound like an English country vicar whose mission is to make the non-religious feel comfortable.

Even Sister Wendy confesses to scurrying past Ruben's *Descent from the Cross*, Titian's *Pietà*, Grünewald's *Crucifixion*. She finds them too painful. But if we scurry past the Crucifixion, we bypass the Resurrection, an act that reduces Easter to coloured eggs, chocolate bunnies and leg of lamb with rosemary.

It would have been easier to bring Mr Aitchison's *Lamb* home. It would sit on a mantlepiece and embarrass no one. I think of that lamb each day as I check on my living lambs, counting them, praising the good mothers. They enchant the visitors, who exclaim: 'Easter lambs'. Agnus Dei indeed.

April 8, 2009

MORE CHOMP THAN CHEW

IT'S not something I'm proud of, but my bite is worse than my bark. I know this for a fact because I'm on my way to my dentist for the second time this week. The beautiful new crown that she fitted last week, the strongest porcelain known to man, made in Sweden, has cracked. It's the replacement for the first crown, which also cracked.

The first crack took place at a wedding dinner at the Pied à Terre restaurant on Charlotte Street. I can honestly say it was the best food I've ever eaten, but at some point I felt a gaping hole in the back of my jaw. It felt like a crater, but, of course, it was only half a crater. The missing piece of manmade molar had gone down as smoothly as a sliver of *foie gras*.

It's a mystery to the Swedish technicians who produce this miracle product, but not to my dentist. She has been telling me for years that I have a very strong bite. More chomp than chew. To hear her describe it, you'd think I was weaned on armadillos. This wasn't always the case. It's only with age that I've morphed into a snapping turtle, which is inconvenient, because old teeth really aren't up to it. But, like a snapping turtle, I find it harder and harder to let go of things. For instance, for months I've been obsessed with Bernard Madoff. You'd think I had invested my own life's savings with the disgraced financier whose Ponzi scheme swindled investors out of millions.

In fact, I'd never even heard of him, never even been to Palm Beach, although I once sat next to Elie Wiesel at a dinner in New York. The Holocaust survivor and Nobel Laureate's Foundation for Humanity lost $15 million, and he now feels sad rage, a feeling I shared as I Googled each evening before bed, typing in 'Madoff victims tell their stories' to stoke my fire.

But disaster and calamity moves at such a pace that while Mr Madoff was still penned up in his penthouse he got pushed aside by bankers' bonuses, as ordained by our inept Government and funded by the humble taxpayer. And while I was snarling over Sir Fred's lifetime-achievement pension, along came the Somalian pirates. Frankly, my reaction to those impoverished men in little boats (who collected £150 million in ransoms last year) shocked even me. 'Kill them,' I blasted over my morning cup of organic Fairtrade coffee. 'They throw grenades at the ships? Throw them back!'

Despite my nightly attempts to figure out how an

Evinrude/Johnson with a crew of four could commandeer a freighter on the high seas, I was stumped. Then my friend Lawrence who works at the International Maritime Organization explained that the freighters fly flags of convenience and have the smallest crews possible. Ransom has been cheaper than armed crews. Oh. Perhaps now, after 78 ships have been attacked, 19 hijacked and more than 300 hostages taken since February, the insurers will rethink.

And where is my sympathy for Somalia, the hotbed of Islamic extremism described by the UN as the 'world's worst humanitarian disaster'? I grind my teeth in despair. Somalia. Zimbabwe. Kenya. South Africa. Darfur. The Congo. Was it always so hopeless? Has it become worse? Is there anything that can be done?

Meanwhile, I have half a crown. I know it is a privileged piece of dentistry. A Swedish crown intact could feed a family in bleakest Africa for a year. Just knowing that makes me feel queasy, because being a white, middle-class country dweller doesn't make you indifferent to the world's troubles. Like snapping turtles, we aren't so well covered by our shells that we're impervious. Actually, snapping turtles are shy creatures, not inclined to look for trouble, but if threatened they will respond with a fierce chomp. Snap.

April 29, 2009

TIMEWATCH

WE didn't watch the finals of *Britain's Got Talent*. Not because we were feeling superior – I watched Susan Boyle's first appearance on YouTube 10 times – but on the night, we were sitting in the garden with Sam, just home from Edinburgh, exams over, filled with the joys of living in a great city, loving his course, planning his summer. By the time we remembered, the final was over. So we watched a repeat of *Timewatch* about D-Day instead.

It focused on Omaha Beach, the toughest and bloodiest battle of the D-Day invasions on the Normandy beaches. I grew up hearing the words Omaha Beach, but the uncles and fathers of friends who were part of the biggest amphibious assault in history never talked about it. I only began piecing the story together 15 years ago, when my closest friend from university days wrote from Massachusetts that she was coming to France with her father for the 50th anniversary of D-Day. It was the first time I knew that Morley Piper, a man I'd known since I was 18 and who'd tolerantly accepted me as a part-time member of his family, was one of the American GIs who landed on Omaha Beach on June 6, 1944.

Images of that first wave of troops in their landing craft were implanted in modern consciousness long before *Saving Private Ryan*. The rows of helmets, the 100lb loads of weapons and supplies on their backs, the metal craft bucking with the waves. I was also vaguely aware that, despite the planning for 'the most important battle in the history of the world', it all went wrong. *Timewatch* spelled out the true horror of the disasters. In the 30 minutes before H-hour, the US Air Force dropped 13,000 tons of bombs. Despite their claims that they could 'put a bomb into a pickle barrel', on D-Day, the bombers, wanting to avoid the oncoming armada, flew across the beaches, completely missing the German machinegunners in bunkers in the bluffs. Unharmed, the Germans would turn the beaches into a scene of slaughter.

Morley Piper, a tall, thin boy from the Midwest, was just 19. He enlisted in his second year of college because he figured that officer training was better than being drafted. But, after only a few months, the training programme was stopped in order to add units for the invasion. Now a second lieutenant and a platoon leader in the 29th Infantry Division, Morley was bound for England and months of training near Southampton.

His memories of D-Day are of the smoke, the fog and the cliffs, where German machinegunners had perfect aim at the waves of troops coming off the ramps. Of the 30 men in his platoon, only 17 made it to shore. Once on the beach, 'our well-crafted plan – to blast our way through the beach defences – became secondary to survival'. There were 300 yards of open sand, no cover, no trees, no trenches. Historians now believe the original estimate of 2,000 dead or missing is closer to 4,500 or 5,000.

Morley decided not to return to France for the 65th anniversary*. A youthful 85-year-old who still works full time as executive director of New England Newspaper & Press Association, he opted to stay home and attend the graduation of his youngest granddaughter. The truth is, despite a Bronze Star and a Purple Heart, Morley doesn't dwell on June 6, 1944, and the months of fighting that followed.

But D-Day's been in my thoughts all week. This morning I bought two copies of Antony Beevor's book *D-Day: The Battle for Normandy*, one for Morley and one for my son, who is the age of so many who died on those beaches. I want him to know about the Americans and Britons who had audacity and bravery. I want him to know the meaning of talent.

June 10, 2009

---

* He made it to the 70th anniversary in 2014, accompanied by his daughters, two granddaughters and great-granddaughter.

COMMON GOOD, COMMON SENSE

THE first of this year's Reith Lectures was held this week in London, and it was my good luck to be there. Not in the BBC Radio Theatre in Broadcasting House, among the great and the good. No, I was in a Volvo V70, sitting in Parliament Square, wedged in between taxis, trucks and vans. All the same, Westminster was probably the right place to be. The title of this year's lectures is 'A New Citizenship', culminating in thoughts on 'A New Politics of the Common Good'.

Michael Sandel is the first Reith Lecturer I've ever heard of. His course on Justice at Harvard is legendary, and last year I watched a video of his lectures on the Harvard website. It showed a rapt audience of 1,200 young faces and the professor, without notes, engaging them on the complex relationship between action and intention. I envied those lucky students.

On the secular stretch of Victoria Street between Westminster Cathedral and Westminster Abbey, Sue

Lawley introduced Prof Sandel's first lecture, 'Markets and Morals'. Market fundamentalism began with Thatcher and Reagan, and was consolidated under Clinton and Blair, disciples who developed the faith that markets are the primary instruments for achieving the common good. It's unnerving to hear the roll call of markets in our daily lives. Private prisons. Carbon trading. Wombs for hire. Kidneys for sale. Ambulances for hire. Even the wars we fight. A year after the invasion, there were more private contractors in Iraq than there were troops. We can blame who we like, but the truth is we're the generation that presided over the transformation of the citizen into a consumer.

While I'm stalled on the bend next to the statue of Nelson Mandela, Prof Sandel addresses carbon trading. If rich countries can 'sell' their pollutants to poor countries, it removes the moral stigma of polluting the air and water. If the airline plants a clump of trees each time you fly to New York, you don't have to feel so guilty. You're buying the right to pollute.

He then tells about a nursery school where the parents were often late collecting their children. A stigma was attached to these parents because their lateness meant that the teachers had to stay late. To improve the situation, fines were introduced for late pick-ups. Guess what happened? The late pick-ups increased. With the fines, late arrival simply became a service the parents were willing to pay for. The fine became a fee, and the fee removed the guilt. Arriving late became morally acceptable.

Although I hang on to Prof Sandel's every word, I also stare at the road ahead. Or, rather, the roadworks. I feel a fool for coming around Parliament Square and Whitehall, because for more than a year now these streets have been clogged with planks, trenches, piles of earth, JCBs and traffic cones, the dismal legacy of the 1991 New Roads and Street Works Act which gave its blessing to the newly privatised utilities to dig up roads whenever they wanted. All that's required is 28 days' notice. The council can't refuse permission, can't even demand that the work be co-ordinated with other digging. And if the work isn't finished on time? A £5,000 fine. Not each day, but *in total*.

The fine has become a fee, which is why on the mile in which I listened to an entire Reith Lecture I counted only nine men in hard hats working on this historic stretch of a great capital city. Why pay workers to work overtime when, for a modest fee, you can disrupt the city for years? By the craters of unmanned roadworks, I could sit down and weep.

And, yet, the persuasive voice of Prof Sandel lingers. I roll down my window and shout: 'Arise, fellow citizens! Repeal the 1991 Roads Act.' No one moves an inch.

June 17, 2009

COUNTRY LIFE

IT'S been a long week down on the farm. Heat slows everything down and the countryside looks like one of those slow-motion scenes in *Elvira Madigan*. Fields of barley the colour of Farrow & Ball Straw barely ripple. The sugar beet, green as a spinach salad a week ago, now looks limp and weary. We'd like to give it a drink, but even the machinery is complaining. Everything mechanical in the pump house has succumbed to heatstroke, causing the irrigation to shudder to a halt.

But it's the animals who really suffer from the heat. Otis has gone off his food and won't budge from a patch in the kitchen where the overhead fan and two open windows resemble a breeze. Minou, a semi-wild barn cat, has decamped to a shady glade by the horse pond. And in the middle of a field that looks as hot as Texas, Norah, matriarch of my small herd of Red Polls, has given birth to a calf.

It's not like we weren't expecting it. For months, she's

looked like she was delivering a Pontiac, and last week she wandered off on her own. What we didn't expect was that her calf, a beautiful girl, would arrive on the hottest day of the year. Despite a low birth weight, she seemed sprightly enough and we figured that all was well. In fact, nothing was well. Age – Norah is 17 – and heat – 91°F – had robbed Norah of her milk. The crucial eight hours when the calf most needs the colostrum had passed, and she never got a drop, surviving entirely on nutrients supplied before she entered this hot world.

It's one of those mysteries in life that, as bombs go off around the world, jobs and homes are lost, and all hell is breaking loose, when an animal's life is at stake everything suddenly stops. Will, who runs the farm, and Ollie, his right-hand man, fully stretched to repair the irrigation, bale the hay, and gear up the combines for harvest, both stop everything to give me a hand in the attempt to save the calf's life. While I caress Norah and hold her still, Ollie gets what milk he can from her, filling the baby bottle from the lambing shed. The calf drinks it and our spirits soar. The difference between life and death is in the sucking. But attempts to get more milk reveal how serious the situation is: Norah's as dry as a bone.

But this is the age of the mobile phone. In minutes, Will and Ollie have called around and found frozen colostrum, prepared for emergencies by Jane Capon who has a herd of Jerseys. An hour later, she arrives with it, and two gallons of fresh organic milk and a vial of Rescue Remedy. We're on our way.

But by 6 o'clock the next morning our optimism seemed far-fetched. A farmer basing decisions on economics wouldn't have called the vet, but by now we'd entered more emotional terrain. At 6:30am, I made the call, and half an hour later the 'cattle' vet arrived. Nigel Swayne looks more like Gary Cooper's sidekick in *High Noon*, always in jeans and a freshly ironed Ralph Lauren shirt, grey-haired, calm, lucid, direct. Farmers all over Suffolk think he's a miracle-worker – and I've witnessed one myself – but Nigel doesn't believe in miracles. He prefers science, although he's always grateful for luck. One look at the listless calf, and he tells us she 'isn't really a runner', but he gives her a couple of injections, begins rehydrating her and shows us how to get the tube inside her mouth, all 12in of it.

And so I move between hope and hope abandoned. Just when I think we should let the patient die quietly, she shows her survivor's spirit. Meanwhile, I'm trying hard not to let the calf's suffering become the embodiment of all the wretchedness on Earth. I don't know if Norah's sad eyes are telling me she's grateful or begging me to leave them in peace. The temperature is rising and life is put on hold*.

July 8, 2009

---

* The calf, named Angelica, is now five years old.

THE FOG OF WAR

SUNDAY evenings during harvest are like the slow movement in a sonata. After the nervous *allegro* of waiting, the combines pull out of the farmyard. As first reports come in – yields high, moisture low – a welcome *andante* descends. We open a bottle of wine, then settle down to left-overs with only the sensitive voice of Matthew Bannister for company, presenting *Last Word*, the weekly obituary programme.

In the week in which eight British soldiers were killed in Afghanistan – and 15 in 10 days – not one of the obituaries is of a British soldier. Perhaps 18-year-olds haven't done enough in their short lives to merit a slot, but I've never heard the obituary of a soldier serving in Iraq or Afghanistan on the show. Even Lt Col Rupert Thorneloe – 1,000 men under his command, highest-ranking soldier to die in this war, a career that saw service in Northern Ireland, Bosnia and Iraq before Afghanistan – didn't make it. But on Sunday evening another former soldier was the lead obituary: Robert S. McNamara, Defense Secretary under Kennedy and Johnson, best known as 'architect of the Vietnam war'.

With his slicked-down hair, steel-rimmed glasses and formidable intellect, McNamara is fixed in the minds of the generation who lived through a futile war in which 58,000 Americans and between two to three million Vietnamese died. Nothing quite prepared me for the genial recollections in *Last Word*. Ted Sorenson described him as 'a thoughtful, forceful, articulate and compassionate friend'. Henry Kissinger insisted that he was 'the executor, not the architect, of the Vietnam war'. But the most compelling was Errol Morris, whose film *The Fog of War* received an Oscar for best documentary. For two hours, the then 85-year-old McNamara was interviewed about his life and the conflict that, by 1964, had come to be known as 'McNamara's War'. Asked if the film was McNamara's *mea culpa*, the film-maker replied: 'No. How do you apologise for history?'

The film's title refers to the uncertainty that hovers over the battlefield during fighting. The format is 'R. S. McNamara's 11 life lessons', inspired by the former Secretary of Defense's list from *In Retrospect: The Tragedy and Lessons of Vietnam*, published in 1995. Lessons that now seem so obvious: failure to understand the enemy, failure to understand the limits of high-tech weapons, failure to tell the truth to the American people – the dangers to our country were exaggerated. Failure to recognise that we don't have a God-given right to shape every nation in our image.

Lulled by the hum of combines, I could forget that this patch of Suffolk is the staging post for war: RAF Honington is three miles from here; Lakenheath and Mildenhall, the two largest US bases in Europe, less than 30 minutes away. By 1966, McNamara knew 'the war in Vietnam was unwinnable', but he couldn't persuade the politicians for whom the pretence of future benefits appears better than admitting loss. Because lives have been lost, no one wants to write off sunken costs.

In 1967, McNamara was fired by President Johnson. Another 42,000 American soldiers would die in the seven years that followed. McNamara is described as wandering around Washington later in life, 'a haunted man'. As I go out to check on the harvest, I wonder who will be the haunted men if we stay in Afghanistan; who, in a quiet and prosperous future, will be unable to apologise for history.

In the heat and dust of the grain store, I remember McNamara's final two lessons of Vietnam. We failed to recognise that in international affairs there may be problems for which there are no solutions. That, at times, we may have to live with an imperfect, untidy world.

July 22, 2009

THE MEANING OF TREASON

WHEN his memory was still intact, Ralph Waldo Emerson wrote: 'We remember that we forget.' With that in mind, I do small inventories to make sure everything is still clicking. I play old exam pieces on the piano. I recite *As Kingfishers Catch Fire*. And, sometimes, to see if I remember, I list the five who spied for Russia.

If I just rolled off the names – Burgess, Philby, Maclean, Blunt and Cairncross – it would be scant proof that my memory is alive, but I do little mental notes. Because of Alan Bennett's *An Englisman Abroad*, Guy Burgess is forever Alan Bates, pudgy, sodden, loathing his grim life in Moscow, longing for his old haunts in St James's, his silk pyjamas from Sulka, his shoes from Lobb. Oppidan, and winner of the Rosebery and Gladstone prizes, at Eton in 1929, the spy was too unpopular to be elected to Pop but won a history scholarship to Trinity College, Cambridge.

Burgess never intended to defect. In 1951, he was considering a request by the Salisbury family to complete a biography of the 3rd Marquess of Salisbury, one of his great heroes, and looking forward to a weekend in Paris with an American he'd met on the *Queen Mary* when he received the news from Anthony Blunt that Maclean was to be interrogated on Monday, May 28. On the Friday, Maclean, son of a Liberal MP, educated at Gresham's Holt and Trinity Hall, Cambridge, was taken out by friends, including Cyril Connolly, for a 'birthday treat' of oysters and Champagne in Soho. In the evening, the 38-year-old spy went home to his wife. Half an hour later, Burgess arrived to tell him that that his escape had to begin. Burgess only planned to accompany Maclean as far as France, but the KGB had other ideas.

These details came back with the news that Blunt's memoir, sealed in a container in the British Library for 25 years, has now been made public. Blunt, Surveyor of The Queen's Pictures, the 'Fourth Man', the talent scout who recruited Burgess. And the subject of another Bennett play, *A Question of Attribution*.

I once felt sympathy for these men. I'd read *A Generation on Trial*, Alistair Cooke's account of the Alger Hiss trial in America when I still thought he was the innocent victim of McCarthyism and anti-Communist fever. But the more that was revealed, the more uneasy I became with the young men drawn to spy for Russia through a combination of ideology, peer pressure, complicated notions of morality and disruptive sexual yearnings. It was one thing to fight in Spain against Fascism, quite another to be operating in MI5 and MI6 after the Hitler-Stalin pact.

Nowhere in his memoir does Blunt express regret at lying to friends, recruiting agents and passing secrets to Moscow. What he regrets is getting found out, being stripped of his knighthood. The fastidious art historian doesn't understand the difference between regret and remorse.

Mr Bennett believed that Blunt should have been allowed to keep his knighthood because the honour was for his 'contribution as an art historian'. He thinks that little evidence exists that 'Blunt did any substantial damage'. His comments infuriated Cooke, who rejected as 'fanciful in the extreme' that Blunt was on the lower rungs of traitorous espionage, that a man's expertise on Poussin 'does not diminish or cushion his responsibility for sending countless decent people to their deaths'.

We will never know the extent of their damage. By learning the West's atomic secrets, the Russians felt capable of arming Kim Il-sung, setting the stage for the Korean War. That's enough to wipe the dreamy look off any account. Or, as Coral Browne, the English actress who meets Guy Burgess in Moscow, put it: 'Outside Shakespeare, the word "treason" to me means nothing – only you pissed in our soup and we drank it.' To re-phrase Emerson, I don't think we should forget to remember.

August 5, 2009

BOOKS: A MEMOIR

WE'RE sitting in the restaurant gazing at the menu, but shyly glancing at one another. We try to remember how long it's been and finally settle on 'more than 20 years', so a mutual inventory is inevitable. Marcia, a few years older, looks younger. She has the look I love – serene chic: a slate-blue Mandarin blouse, a double-strand silver necklace. She looks like an Eileen Fisher ad.

After we order, we skim through the missing decades. She's now a grandmother, her only daughter married to a lawyer who's on the staff of a senator I admire. Her father, a former US ambassador and Cold War warrior, left the beautiful family farm in Middleburg, Virginia, to a foundation dedicated to his memory, a blow (I imagine) to his four children. But Marcia doesn't dwell on regrets. After her marriage ended, she started a second-hand bookshop in Georgetown, the ancient, leafy section of Washington. Her business partner was the novelist Larry McMurtry, who shared Marcia's passion for tracking down, buying and selling books: the good, the rare, the irreplaceable. Called Booked Up, the bookshop was an institution in a city full of booklovers. I still have the books I bought there: Hemingway's *A Moveable Feast*, Flannery O'Connor's *A Good Man is Hard to Find*.

Marcia's shop was a place of pilgrimage, the perfect blend of antiquarian and second-hand, with the woody smell of acid-free paper, the peace of timeless browsing, the bliss of discovering haveable treasures. When I heard that it had closed, after 35 successful years, I grieved even though I live 3,000 miles away.

'They're all disappearing now,' she tells me. First, it was the landlords who want a Starbucks or a mobile-phone shop, proof the neighbourhood is on the up. But the deadly arrow was the internet.

'It began with Amazon,' Marcia says. Suddenly, people could go online. Amazon beat the publishers down, had low rent and staff costs. Precise, efficient, cheap and fast. But not the serendipitous and out of print. Then, along came www.alibris.com and www.abebooks.com, the online survival kit for used-book sellers. The sellers soon discovered that they no longer needed the little shop with the bell on the door and the cat in the window. All that was required was postage scales, Jiffy bags and a willingness to catalogue books and drive to the post office. Within five years, one of the most appealing pillars of the civilised world had vanished.

I confess my guilt to Marcia. When I first discovered Amazon, it seemed like a miracle: the isolation of country life was over and the books arriving in their brown cartons felt like presents. Until a 42in flat-screen TV was charged to my Amazon account by someone in Liverpool. Untangling the fraud was hell. I cancelled my 1-Click account and transferred my affection to www.abebooks.com. Midnight prowls, searching for long-lost books, became an addiction. I comforted myself with the knowledge that www.abebooks.com consisted of thousands of used-book sellers.

Marcia then warns me of another threat more terrible to the world of books than all the above. The Kindle and other wireless reading devices. 'But people will never forego the sheer pleasure of rippling the pages, sniffing, owning a book,' I say.

'But if you can carry around 300,000 books, your newspaper – and probably COUNTRY LIFE – in your handbag?' She looks at me. 'Remember when we wrote letters? Now, we send emails. And we collected records and CDs? We now have iPods. Waterstones has sold 30,000 Sony Readers this year.'

Last year, Mr McMurtry wrote a meditation on modern reading habits. In it, he said that 'the complex truth is that many activities last for centuries, and then simply (or unsimply) stop'. Go out and buy it while you can. It's called *Books: A Memoir*.

August 12, 2009

THE SNOW GOOSE PROPHECY

IT began with the Hudson Bay blanket my grandmother sent me my first term at university. I wrote to her about the first snowfall, describing the exotic world of icicles and snow banks, the novelty of sleeping in socks and sweaters. Two weeks later, a thick wool blanket arrived, white with four stripes in green, red, yellow and indigo. 'The English settlers used these blankets to trade with the Indians in exchange for beaver pelts,' she wrote, 'but the blankets aren't made in Hudson's Bay but in England, and the point system – yours is a four point – doesn't refer to its value in pelts, as commonly believed, but to its size and thickness.' She enclosed a map of Canada. Written beneath the words Hudson's Bay, in her blue-black ink, was 'breeding ground for snow geese'.

My Hudson Bay blanket kept me warm for the next four years. It also reignited my passion for snow geese, a passion that had begun in my childhood when I once saw them flying over the Delta and heading up the Mississippi River, their highway up north. Their appearance seemed as carefully organised as a homecoming parade. They arrived on time, in V formation, in such vast numbers that, after half an hour, it felt more like an eclipse than a migratory miracle.

Reverence for snow geese was instilled in me on that day. I was told that they mate for life and are devoted parents, staying with their offspring on the first migration south. They keep together during the winter, and return to the breeding ground in Hudson Bay *en famille*, the male leading the family in flight, 'unlike ducks, where the female takes the lead'.

Then, life moved on. I gave my Hudson Bay blanket to a nephew, along with a tear-stained copy of Paul Gallico's *The Snow Goose* and my copy of *Water Birds of North America*. A few years ago, however, in a nostalgic moment, I bought a linocut of snow geese by Robert Gillmor; and last spring, on a visit to Cornwall, I stayed up all night reading a book called *The Snow Geese* by William Fiennes. The English writer follows the snow geese on their migration north, starting in Texas and travelling all the way to Foxe Land, north of Hudson's Bay. Travel book and naturalist's guide, it's also a meditation on 'home' – its importance, not only to humans, but to many other species.

Missing from *The Snow Geese* was the botanist Robert Jefferies. Like Mr Fiennes, Prof Jefferies was born in England, and, like the writer, he became fascinated by snow geese. In 1975, Prof Jefferies left the University of

East Anglia to spend a year as visiting professor at the University of Toronto. He then spent the next 30 years in Canada, studying nesting snow geese at Hudson Bay. One of the earliest scientists to record the exploding population of snow geese, Prof Jefferies traced the change to farmers in the south, who were cultivating more and more land and no longer ploughing fields in autumn, thus providing the geese with ample meals of wheat, soybeans and maize. The well-fed birds were in better shape for their long journey and for breeding. However, once the foraging birds reached the Arctic regions, they were stripping the salt marshes of their vegetation, causing seawater to seep into the marshes, which in turn increased the reflectivity to the sun, making the temperatures rise. The snow geese were contributing to global warming.

Prof Jefferies' discovery won him a Nobel Prize. He was part of the UN panel on Climate Change that shared the prize with Al Gore in 2007. Before he died last week of a cerebral haemorrhage, Prof Jefferies revealed how increased use of fertilisers was having the same effect on salt marshes in Europe. His work on snow geese says more about humans than about the birds he loved. On this farm we've just completed our harvest, a whole month earlier than we did when I arrived here in 1986. Call it the snow geese prophecy.

August 19, 2009

TRUTH *VS.* MERCY

LOOKING back, it was an almost perfect week. Luminous days spent in Cumbria with friends who provided princely hospitality: rooms oozing with comfort and sweet peas and lavender; dinners of their own salt-marsh lamb and tender broad beans; breakfasts 'at 9ish' in a sunny dining room with strong coffee, scrambled eggs, bacon as crisp as parchment and a quartet of newspapers. And that true element of lavishness: their time. We explored the estate, picnicked in an abandoned farmstead by the sea, and wandered in the garden, accompanied by four lurchers as enchanting and inexplicable as Marlene Dietrich.

We left restored and exhilarated, reliving the hours on the drive home, speaking above the fuzzy, cake-filled soundtrack of the Test match on the car radio.

Other joys of the week: the Proms, listening to a concert performance of *Fidelio*, with Daniel Barenboim conducting the West-Eastern Divan Orchestra, a humanitarian miracle of young Arab and Jewish musicians. And, the next day, another miracle: England regaining the Ashes. By evening I had emerged from my Test cricket coma and watched the replays. My husband wept.

And so, the summer eases away, apples already carpeting the orchard, the garden seeding and tall. All these things. And one more. This was the week that the Lockerbie bomber Abdelbaset al-Megrahi was released. That, 'in the name of compassion', the terminally ill terrorist returned to his homeland.

Although I'll remember the picnic overlooking the sands of Morecambe Bay, I wonder if I'll recall the heated talk over lunch about the rights and wrongs of freeing the unrepentant murderer of entirely innocent human beings. As we chewed over the words 'mercy' and 'repentance', another guest picked away at the bone of truth: this was compassion without repentance, that, in the name of mercy, only the path to the vast reserves of Libyan gas and oil would be smoothed.

'But we have to watch our step,' he added, and told us of Col Gaddafi's reaction when his son Hannibal and daughter-in-law were arrested last year in Switzerland. Charged with abusing two servants, they were released on bail after two days, but Switzerland is still paying the price for incurring the Libyan leader's wrath: all Swiss flights to Tripoli have been stopped, trade sanctions imposed, more than £5 billion withdrawn from Swiss banks and, despite unctuous apologies from the Swiss government, Libya's crude-oil exports that provide half of Switzerland's oil have been cut.

And here lies the shadow. How willing are we to sell our national souls for oil? As citizens, we quietly accept that self-interest is the survival instinct of nations. What's harder to swallow are lies. Perhaps we weren't aware that the Scottish government leader Alex Salmond was once an oil economist for a Scottish bank, but we know that yields of Scottish oil are declining. Therefore, to be told that 'humanity is a defining characteristic of Scotland' and that the only motive for freeing al-Megrahi was compassion for a dying man feels like moral fraud.

The release of the only man convicted of the Lockerbie bombing is a good moment for soul-searching. Just how dependent do we want to be on Libyan/Russian/Saudi oil? What do we mean by 'justice' and 'mercy'? For some, the release of al-Megrahi may already feel like old news. For those who lost sons and daughters over Lockerbie the injustice is irreversible. Now the only justice to be had is to learn. We should beware of setting aside the law, beware of embracing expediency and calling it 'mercy'. We honour the innocents who fell from the sky that December night by waking up. By deciding what kind of country we want to be.

September 2, 2009

THE HABITAT ADVENT

I DON'T believe it would be overly dramatic to say that my life was changed by an Advent calendar. The year was 1979, and it was my first-ever Advent calendar. I bought it in Habitat on the King's Road and it was predictable Habitat: non-sectarian good taste. I was living in Paris at the time, in an artist's *atelier* behind Montparnasse, and my life was like an ENO production of *La bohème* set in the late seventies. Trips to London – an eight-hour journey in those days – always included an evening at the theatre, a lunch at Cranks, dinner at the Star of India in South Kensington, and shopping: Peter Jones, Laura Ashley, John Sandoe and Habitat. Everything was so much cheaper than in Paris.

Back to the Advent calendar. It was a triptych that opened to reveal the interior of a house on Christmas Day. Downstairs in the kitchen, still in her dressing gown, the mother is lifting a turkey out of the oven of a cream AGA. Behind her, the dog stretches in his basket. On the painted dresser, platters and teapots. On the pine table, a tray of mince pies and two glasses of red wine.

Upstairs, the father, still in pyjamas, sits on the edge of the four-poster bed holding the new baby. At his feet, a Moses basket. And making their way down the stairs, two little girls, gazing at the Christmas tree surrounded by presents. Fire in the fireplace, books on bookshelves, hi-fi with one of those clear plastic covers over the turntable. Bows of ivy over the pictures. A wicker log basket. I could go on, but you get the picture. Home. Familial bliss. Married life. Real furniture. Nice stuff. Good children.

You may wonder why I have such vivid recall of an Advent calendar that goes back 30 years. Two reasons. That Advent calendar became a kind of icon for me. Suddenly, my liberated and nomadic life seemed as bleak and vast as the Moon. Diatribes about marriage as an oppressive institution suddenly sounded like a script from a dated play. As I studied the rooms in the Advent house, I felt an admiration for people who, despite the trembling uncertainty of life, wanted to create a home, plant trees, breed babies. Instead of seeing the nuclear family as suffocating, it felt like an affirmation of life. The pictures spoke to me of the tender optimism of the human condition.

But from my Damascene revelation – that home and family are fertile fields for nurturing the kind of faith in the ultimate goodness of man that gives us our inner security – to the moment when, in my dressing gown, stepping over

348

the dog to hoist a turkey from the AGA, spilling turkey grease on new slippers while the husband cradles the baby and reads P. G. Wodehouse at the same time, between the concept and the fulfilment, there was a long wait. Ten years.

But waiting is what Advent is about. Waiting, as Ronald Blythe puts it, for the human child who is 'to become one of us to show us what we could be, what we should be'. The year I bought the Advent calendar on the King's Road, I was, to be honest, more interested in Beckett's *Waiting for Godot* than I was in the solemn countdown to the birth of a child in a manger. The words of the Advent Collect, which entreats God to 'give us grace that we may cast away the works of darkness', were still lodged in my memory, but a calendar with a tender-eyed donkey and a babe in swaddling clothes wouldn't have been life-changing.

The other reason I can describe the Habitat Advent calendar is that it's taped permanently to the back door of the larder. Like icons of old, it's there to remind me of its place in the life I have. I have other Advent calendars, including a much-loved collection by Matthew Rice, but this is the one that brought me to Wyken and to this back page. The Habitat Advent. The King's Road. A modest miracle.

November 25, 2009

STAY HUNGRY, STAY FOOLISH

LOST in the attic, behind a wall of green *Hansards*, are my copies of the *Whole Earth Catalog*. I'm pretty sure I have the very first one, published in 1969, with the first satellite image of the Earth as seen from space in the centre of the vast black cover.

Unlike L. L. Bean, the *Whole Earth Catalog* didn't actually sell anything. Its mission was to show readers how and where to find everything, a forerunner of Google, a kind of hippie COUNTRY LIFE for the vast numbers of disenchanted urban dwellers who wanted to go back to the land. Its readers weren't in search of a country estate with 1000 acres, however. They were more likely to be looking for the simple life, assisted by marijuana and casual sex, nurtured by that most useful fertiliser, a trust fund.

I studied with serious purpose entries that showed me how to raise my own barley and make Tibetan barley bread, how to make adobe bricks out of molasses powder and bunker oil, capture a colony of bees and arrange a do-it-yourself burial for $50. Making my own hashish pipe didn't interest me, but I circled the address for a snake-bite kit for $3.

But, despite my hours spent browsing the *Catalog*, I felt no longing to go back to the land. The triumph of my life was getting *off* the land, of knowing that when I walked out my door I was unlikely to need a snake-bite kit ever again. It is with wistful irony I find myself now growing barley. I've put down deep roots, but I neither churn nor weave. My bucolic rambles are now confined to the *Farmers Guardian*, a weekly feed at the trough of despond, and the Thriplow Farms newsletter, an end-of-year account of the farming year written by friend and fellow farmer in Cambridgeshire Oliver Walston.

Oliver is an exotic farmer in these parts. Son of a Labour peer and an American mother, whose 10-year relationship with Graham Greene inspired *The End of the Affair*, Oliver has a rough glamour that is rare in arable country. Despite his education – Eton, Cambridge, Princeton – he isn't a shootin' and fishin' landowner, but a dedicated and cunning farmer. He's also the best chronicler of agricultural life this country has.

His 2009 newsletter arrived this morning. It begins: 'In 2008 we made more money than we have ever made in my farming lifetime. Wheat yields were big, prices higher than ever and costs relatively low. This year we shall lose more money than we have ever lost. Wheat yields were average, prices were down 40% whilst the cost of inputs doubled.'

Those lines gave me the shakes. If Oliver Walston is losing money with all his equipment and know-how (he was the first farmer I knew to have a computer; he always has the latest, biggest kit), what chance do the rest of us have? But he explains the problem. Farming today has nothing to do with husbandry. What separates the good from the bad – and the rich from the poor – is marketing. It's not enough to get the agronomy right: you have to second-guess the rainfall in Australia, the price of oil, currency exchange rates and the capricious moods of a small gang of commodity traders. You then speculate as to when to sell 'forward' (that's where he went wrong in 2009) and when to hang on. Farming, like hedge funds, is a crap shoot.

But hedge funds may be less risky. HSBC predicts that in 2010 it will cost the average farmer £135 to produce a ton of wheat. The forward price this week is £109. The only other farmer I knew near Thriplow sold up to folks whose main crop is concrete – science parks, housing estates, Tescos – and bought a few thousand acres and a salmon river in Scotland. I'm glad that Oliver, like us, is ploughing on. We may not turn our barley into Tibetan bread, but we hold fast to the *Whole Earth* farmer's slingshot of a motto: 'Stay hungry, stay foolish.'

December 9, 2009

A MOVEABLE FEAST

WE promised to love, comfort and honour each other to the end of our days. We also said we would cherish and be faithful always, for richer for poorer, in sickness and in health, at a time in our lives when heart bypasses and new hips were beyond our imaginative powers. And, as if those vows weren't extravagant enough, I held out for more; and, in the rash way of premarital promises, the bridegroom agreed. 'Yes,' he said. 'We will always spend Christmas at home.'

As ours was a spring courtship and a summer wedding, it might seem a quixotic prenuptial contract, but soon after we got engaged the youngest of my three future sisters-in-law explained the Three-Year Plan: every third Christmas in Warwickshire with my husband's oldest sister and her family; the following year, everyone here at Wyken; the year after, half of the family here at Wyken. Eager as I was to embrace the traditions of my new family, the idea of the Carlisle Christmas Rota made me moody as a woodchuck.

My longing for a fixed Nativity began in the backseat of childhood, listening to my parents snap at each other and at us. They were worn out from the effort to disguise things that were meant to arrive on a sleigh, frazzled by the challenge of fitting it all into the boot and, no doubt, wondering why, year after year, they left the home they had created and hauled their hopes and fears of all the years 200 miles north in order to 'go home for Christmas'.

The belief that Christmas is about Family is drip-fed into us from birth; but, in this age of ever-changing families, Place is the scaffolding that provides the sense of permanence and togetherness. If your joy and sustenance is derived from fir trees, log fires and carols that begin at 3pm on Christmas Eve from King's College, Cambridge, it's hard to believe it's Christmas in a hammock under palm trees. Place is as firmly fixed in the mind as the Angel Gabriel, the Shepherds, the Three Wise Men and animals peering into the manger.

But our faith in Place should come with a warning. It is transitory. Cousins who have spent every Christmas of their married lives in North Wales are on their own this year, their son and daughter in London with new in-laws. Friends in Scotland are also having a 'quiet Christmas', their married daughters and grandchildren joining their husbands' families. Suffolk neighbours have a full house, but their Christmas star, daughter Kate, is in India with friends. Everyone is trying not to be morose about these changes.

354

For some, these transitions mean arrival. This will be the first year Caroline gets to 'do' Christmas in the family pile, because her mother-in-law is going to her daughter's family, thereby passing on, at last, the mantle of Mother Christmas.

I'm astonished at the good grace with which my parents accepted my own defection from the Christmas pilgrimage, although every autumn of my unmarried life I received a letter from my father that began, 'Christmas isn't a command performance, but just know we'd be so glad to see you that we'll pay for your ticket'. I'm equally amazed at how casually I made other plans. But when I told him my husband had promised me freedom from the Christmas rota, his September letter took on a different tone. 'Family is a delicate web,' he wrote. 'The strings are strong, but they can be torn apart. Think of the Carlisle rota as a well-worn tapestry and enjoy it. It won't last for ever. I used to dread Christmas at my in-laws. Now, I'd love to relive one.'

My father typed his letters but he always scribbled a postscript. On this letter, he added a nugget that makes me smile as we load the car on Christmas Eve: 'One more thing. Christmas itself is by grace. So lighten up.'

December 23, 2009

355

ACKNOWLEDGEMENTS

Many people have put up with me as I tried to make enough sense of the world to be able to press SEND by noon every Wednesday. For their patience, efficiency, sharp eyes and humour I want to thank Octavia Pollock and Jane Watkins.

For keeping the Wyken show on the road when I was holed up with the deadline, I've been lucky to have Sue Duff, Sarah Patterson, Will Reed, Trevor Pollard and Angie Burrows in my life.

Two old friends who inspired me over many years died before I gathered these pages together: Will McLain and Jorn Langberg.

I miss them.

Two new friends, Lisa Fouché and Mary Gallant, came into my life by way of these columns, and their generosity and praise have kept me at my desk.

I owe my editor Mark Hedges more than I can ever acknowledge. He allowed me to buck and snort on a subject of my choice for so many years.

Wyken is a farming community that goes back to Domesday. Before the war, 40 men and their families lived on this farm. Now agricultural accountants say that a man and a half can farm 1000 acres (although half-men are rare in these parts). When we planted the vineyard and converted our 400-year-old tithe barn into a shop and restaurant, we unwittingly restored life to a rural community. We now have 50 people on the payroll, all of whom are local. I begin every day of my life feeling grateful to the gardeners, chefs, front-of-house and shop staff. The health and happiness of this farm rests on their shoulders.

Producing a column can lead writers to think everything they say is important and true. Sam Carlisle prevented me from falling into that trap by providing regular reality-checks. He also made sure the laughter level at home was maintained at a healthy temperature.

Kenneth Carlisle brought me to Wyken and shared my dreams and schemes to move it into the 21st century. He planted a vineyard despite a preference for whisky, and endured the cows that trampled his wildflower meadows. His company has made these years the happiest of my life.

Columnists write on the sand. It is a transient art, and it's rare for our thoughts to have a second life between hard covers. It wouldn't have happened this time without Marion and Alan Marshall of Mascot Media, who did everything but write it. My gratitude to them is beyond words.